Microsoft® Windows

Sarah E. Hutchinson

Glen J. Coulthard

THE ADVANTAGE SERIES FOR COMPUTER EDUCATION

Irwin
McGraw-Hill

Boston, Massachusetts Burr Ridge, Illinois Dubuque, Iowa
Madison, Wisconsin New York, New York San Francisco, California St. Louis, Missouri

Irwin/McGraw-Hill

*A Division of The **McGraw·Hill** Companies*

MICROSOFT® WINDOWS NT 4.0

6 7 8 9   WC/WC 9 0

ISBN 0-256-26338-8

Publisher: *Tom Casson*
Sponsoring editor: *Garrett Glanz*
Developmental editor: *Kristin Hepburn*
GTS production coordinator: *Cathy Stotts*
Marketing manager: *James Rogers*
Senior project supervisor: *Denise Santor-Mitzit*
Production supervisor: *Pat Frederickson*
Art director: *Keith McPherson*
Prepress buyer: *Heather D. Burbridge*
Compositor: *GTS Graphics, Inc.*
Typeface: *11/13 Bodoni Book*
Printer: *Webcrafters, Inc.*

http://www.mhcollege.com

WELCOME TO THE IRWIN ADVANTAGE SERIES

The Irwin Advantage Series has evolved over the years to become one of the most respected resources for software training in the world—to date, over 200,000 students have used one or more of our learning guides. Our instructional methodologies are proven to optimize the student's ability to learn, yet we continually seek ways to improve on our products and approach. To this end, all of our learning guides are classroom tested and critically reviewed by dozens of learners, teachers, and software training experts. We're glad you have chosen the Irwin Advantage Series!

KEY FEATURES

The following features are incorporated into the new Microsoft Office 97 student learning guides to ensure that your learning experience is as productive and enjoyable as possible:

CASE STUDIES

Each session begins with a real-world **case study** that introduces you to a fictitious person or company and describes their immediate problem or opportunity. Throughout the session, you obtain the knowledge and skills necessary to meet these challenges. At the end of the session, you are given an opportunity to solve **case problems** directly related to the case scenario.

CONCEPTS, SKILLS AND PROCEDURES

Each learning guide organizes and presents its content in logically structured session topics. Commands and procedures are introduced using **hands-on examples in a step-by-step format,** and students are encouraged to perform the steps along with the guide. These examples are clearly identified by the text design.

PERFORM THE FOLLOWING STEPS

Using this new design feature, the step progression for all hands-on examples and exercises are clearly identified. Students will find it surprisingly easy to follow the logical sequence of keystrokes and mouse clicks. No longer do you have to worry about missing a step!

END OF SESSION EXERCISES

Each session concludes with **short answer questions** and **hands-on exercises.** These comprehensive and meaningful exercises are integrated with the session's objectives; they were not added as an afterthought. They serve to provide students with opportunities to practice the session material. For maximum benefit, students should complete all the exercises at the end of each session.

IN ADDITION BOXES

These content boxes are placed strategically throughout the guide and provide information on related topics that are beyond the scope of the current discussion. For example, there are three typical categories that are visually identified by the following icons:

Integration

The key to productive and efficient use of Office 97 is in the integration features for sharing data among the applications. With a few mouse clicks, for example, you can create a PowerPoint presentation from a Word document, copy an Access database into an Excel workbook, and incorporate professional Office Art into your annual report. Under this heading, you will find methods for sharing information among the Microsoft Office 97 applications.

Advanced

In a 200+-page learning guide, there are bound to be features that are important but beyond the scope of the text. Therefore, we call attention to these features and offer suggestions on how to apply techniques or to search for more information.

Internet

The Internet is fast becoming a standard tool for gathering and exchanging information. Office 97 provides a high level of Internet connectivity, allowing the user to draw upon its vast resources and even publish documents directly on the World Wide Web. Although not every student will have a persistent Internet connection, you can review the content under this heading to learn about Office's Internet features.

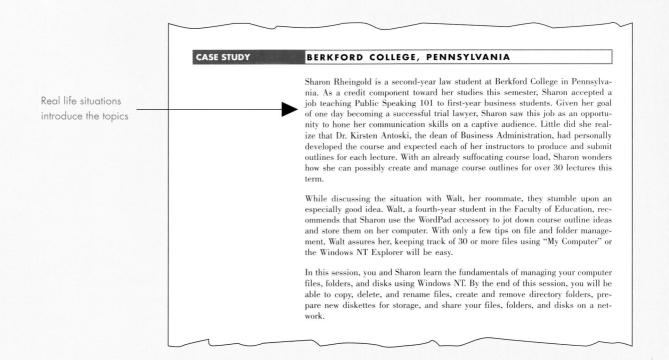

Real life situations introduce the topics

CASE STUDY	BERKFORD COLLEGE, PENNSYLVANIA

Sharon Rheingold is a second-year law student at Berkford College in Pennsylvania. As a credit component toward her studies this semester, Sharon accepted a job teaching Public Speaking 101 to first-year business students. Given her goal of one day becoming a successful trial lawyer, Sharon saw this job as an opportunity to hone her communication skills on a captive audience. Little did she realize that Dr. Kirsten Antoski, the dean of Business Administration, had personally developed the course and expected each of her instructors to produce and submit outlines for each lecture. With an already suffocating course load, Sharon wonders how she can possibly create and manage course outlines for over 30 lectures this term.

While discussing the situation with Walt, her roommate, they stumble upon an especially good idea. Walt, a fourth-year student in the Faculty of Education, recommends that Sharon use the WordPad accessory to jot down course outline ideas and store them on her computer. With only a few tips on file and folder management, Walt assures her, keeping track of 30 or more files using "My Computer" or the Windows NT Explorer will be easy.

In this session, you and Sharon learn the fundamentals of managing your computer files, folders, and disks using Windows NT. By the end of this session, you will be able to copy, delete, and rename files, create and remove directory folders, prepare new diskettes for storage, and share your files, folders, and disks on a network.

Large figures guide
learning

Easy to read and
identify step-by-step
instructions

In Addition boxes
expand on topics

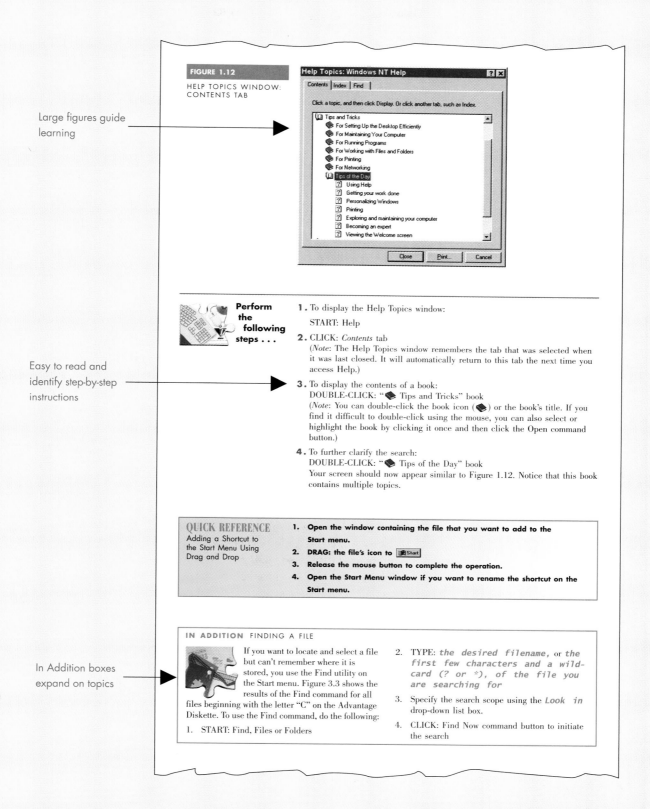

FIGURE 1.12

HELP TOPICS WINDOW:
CONTENTS TAB

**Perform
the
following
steps . . .**

1. To display the Help Topics window:
START: Help

2. CLICK: *Contents* tab
(*Note*: The Help Topics window remembers the tab that was selected when
it was last closed. It will automatically return to this tab the next time you
access Help.)

3. To display the contents of a book:
DOUBLE-CLICK: "◆ Tips and Tricks" book
(*Note*: You can double-click the book icon (◆) or the book's title. If you
find it difficult to double-click using the mouse, you can also select or
highlight the book by clicking it once and then click the Open command
button.)

4. To further clarify the search:
DOUBLE-CLICK: "◆ Tips of the Day" book
Your screen should now appear similar to Figure 1.12. Notice that this book
contains multiple topics.

QUICK REFERENCE
Adding a Shortcut to
the Start Menu Using
Drag and Drop

**1. Open the window containing the file that you want to add to the
Start menu.**

2. DRAG: the file's icon to 🔲Start

3. Release the mouse button to complete the operation.

**4. Open the Start Menu window if you want to rename the shortcut on the
Start menu.**

IN ADDITION FINDING A FILE

If you want to locate and select a file
but can't remember where it is
stored, you use the Find utility on
the Start menu. Figure 3.3 shows the
results of the Find command for all
files beginning with the letter "C" on the Advantage
Diskette. To use the Find command, do the following:

1. START: Find, Files or Folders

2. TYPE: *the desired filename*, or *the
    first few characters and a wild-
    card (? or *), of the file you
    are searching for*

3. Specify the search scope using the *Look in*
    drop-down list box.

4. CLICK: Find Now command button to initiate
    the search

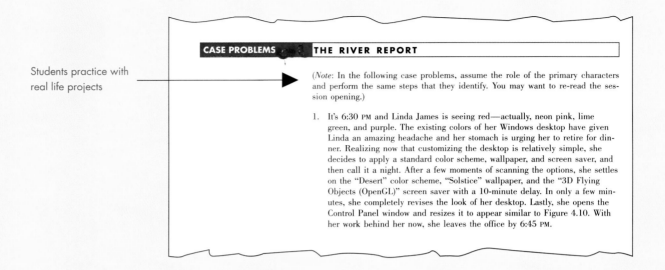

Students practice with
real life projects

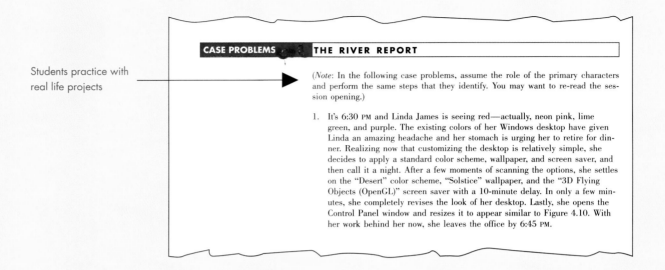

CASE PROBLEMS | THE RIVER REPORT

(*Note*: In the following case problems, assume the role of the primary characters
and perform the same steps that they identify. You may want to re-read the session opening.)

1. It's 6:30 PM and Linda James is seeing red—actually, neon pink, lime
   green, and purple. The existing colors of her Windows desktop have given
   Linda an amazing headache and her stomach is urging her to retire for dinner. Realizing now that customizing the desktop is relatively simple, she
   decides to apply a standard color scheme, wallpaper, and screen saver, and
   then call it a night. After a few moments of scanning the options, she settles
   on the "Desert" color scheme, "Solstice" wallpaper, and the "3D Flying
   Objects (OpenGL)" screen saver with a 10-minute delay. In only a few minutes, she completely revises the look of her desktop. Lastly, she opens the
   Control Panel window and resizes it to appear similar to Figure 4.10. With
   her work behind her now, she leaves the office by 6:45 PM.

TEXT SUPPLEMENTS

ADVANTAGE FILES

Certain hands-on examples and exercises are marked with a disk ◆ icon, indi-
cating the need to retrieve a document file from the **Advantage Files location.**
These document files may be provided to you in a number of ways: packaged
on a diskette accompanying this text, or on the computer network at your school.
You may also download the files from the ***Advantage Online*** Web site
(http://www.irwin.com/cit/adv). *These document files are extremely important to your
success.* Check with your instructor or lab advisor for details on how to acquire the
Advantage Files.

In addition to identifying the Advantage Files location, you will also need to specify a **Data Files location.** This location is used to save the documents that you
create and may either be a blank diskette or a folder on the network server. Again,
your instructor or lab advisor will specify the proper locations. More information
on the file locations and the proper techniques for retrieving and saving information is provided inside the back cover of this book.

CD-ROM INTERACTIVE TUTORIALS

In addition to using this book, you may have access to our *Advantage Interactive* software. These interactive multimedia tutorials are fully integrated with the
material from each session and make effective use of video clips, screen demon-
strations, hands-on exercises, and quizzes. You will enjoy the opportunity to
explore these tutorials and learn the software at your own pace. For ordering information, please refer to the coupon inside the front cover.

INSTRUCTOR'S RESOURCE KIT

For instructors and software trainers, each learning guide is accompanied by an **Instructor's Resource Kit (IRK).** This kit provides suggested answers to the short-answer questions, hands-on exercises, and case problems appearing at the end of each session. Furthermore, the IRK includes a comprehensive test bank of additional short-answer, multiple-choice, and fill-in-the-blank questions, plus hands-on exercises. You will also find a diskette copy of the Advantage Files which may be duplicated or placed on your network for student use.

SUPPORT THROUGH THE WWW

The Internet, and more specifically the World Wide Web, is an important component in our approach to software instruction for the Office 97 application series. The *Advantage Online* site at http://www.irwin.com/cit/adv is a tremendous resource for all users, providing information on the latest software and learning guide releases, download options for the Advantage Files, and supplemental files for the Instructor Resource Kits. We also introduce new methods for you to communicate with the authors, publisher, and other users of the series. As a dynamic venture, *Advantage Online* will evolve and improve over time. Please visit us to see the latest developments and contribute your valuable feedback.

NETWORK TESTING

Evaluation and assessment are important components of any instructional series. We are committed to providing quality alternatives to traditional testing instruments. With our Irwin Network Test Interactive software, instructors can select questions, create and administer tests, and then calculate grades—all on-line! Visit the *Advantage Online* site for more information on how we are progressing in this exciting area.

BEFORE YOU BEGIN

As with any software instruction guide, there are standard conventions that we use to indicate menu options, keystroke combinations, and command instructions.

MENU INSTRUCTIONS

In Office 97, all Menu bar options and pull-down menu commands have an underlined or highlighted letter in each option. When you need to execute a command from the Menu bar—the row of menu choices across the top of the screen—the tutorial's instruction line separates the Menu bar option from the command with a comma. Notice also that the word "CHOOSE" is always used for menu commands. For example, the command for quitting Windows is shown as:

CHOOSE: File, Exit

This instruction tells you to choose the File option on the Menu bar and then to choose the Exit command from the File pull-down menu. The actual steps for choosing a menu command are discussed later in this guide.

KEYSTROKES AND KEYSTROKE COMBINATIONS

When two keys must be pressed together, the tutorial's instruction line shows the keys joined with a plus (+) sign. For example, you can execute a Copy command in Windows by holding down `CTRL` and then pressing the letter c.

The instruction for this type of keystroke combination follows:

PRESS: `CTRL`+c

COMMAND INSTRUCTIONS

This guide indicates with a special typeface and color the data that you are required to type in yourself. For example:

TYPE: Income Statement

When you are required to enter unique information, such as the current date or your name, the instruction appears in italic. The following instruction directs you to type your name in place of the actual words: "your name."

TYPE: *your name*

ACKNOWLEDGMENTS

This series of learning guides is the direct result of the teamwork and heart of many people. We sincerely thank the reviewers, instructors, and students who have shared their comments and suggestions with us over the past few years. We do read them! With this valuable feedback, our guides have evolved into the product you see before you. We also appreciate the efforts of the instructors and students at Okanagan University College who classroom tested our guides to ensure accuracy, relevancy, and completeness.

We also give many thanks to Garrett Glanz, Kristin Hepburn and Tom Casson from Irwin for their skillful management of this text. In fact, special recognition goes to all of the individuals mentioned in the credits at the beginning of this guide. And finally, to the many others who weren't directly involved in this project but who have stood by us the whole way, we appreciate your encouragement and support.

WRITE TO US

We welcome your response to this book, for we are trying to make it as useful a learning tool as possible. Write to us in care of Garrett Glanz, Richard D. Irwin, 1333 Burr Ridge Parkway, Burr Ridge, IL 60521. Thank you.

Sarah E. Hutchinson
sclifford@mindspring.com

Glen J. Coulthard
current@junction.net

Contents

SESSION 1
Fundamentals

SESSION 2
Using WordPad and Other Accessories

SESSION 3
Managing Files and Disks

SESSION 4
Customizing Windows

APPENDIX
Microsoft Windows NT 4.0: Advanced Topics

Microsoft Windows NT 4.0

Fundamentals

SESSION

1

SESSION OUTLINE

INTRODUCTION

Welcome to Windows NT, Microsoft's most powerful operating system for the personal computer. An operating system is the software program that runs the computer. It is the first program loaded when the computer is turned on and, without it, you cannot use your applications software. Understanding how to use Windows NT will help you get the most out of your computer. This session gets you started with the basics.

| CASE STUDY | CITY OF ALBERTVILLE, NEW YORK |

The City of Albertville actively supports the summer job club that is organized by the local high school. In fact, the City hires several students from the school each summer. Besides handling the filing and copying duties in the office, students are responsible for entering data and generating reports using personal computers. The high school does not have adequate computer facilities and, therefore, the hands-on experience provided by the City is extremely valuable to the students.

Ralph Klein, Samantha Yoshi, and Kyra Elmore were very enthusiastic about their first day of work. They had all received word two weeks ago, after intensive interviews, that they had been chosen as the successful applicants for three openings in the Planning and Mapping Department. Arriving at 8:00 AM in the main foyer of City Hall, they were ushered into a second-floor meeting room to await the arrival of their new supervisor, Buzz Pringle. In addition to being the department manager, Buzz was a well-respected civil engineer and a long-time employee with the city.

"Welcome to the City of Albertville's Planning and Mapping Department." Buzz spoke loudly as he entered the room and extended a hand to each of his new employees in turn. "I'd like to take a few minutes to bring you up to speed with what's been happening in my department. Last week, we moved our computer-assisted drafting or CAD operators to a Windows NT version of their software. You must understand that these are people who have never used Windows in their lives! Your initial job will be to help my CAD operators understand the benefits of using Windows and to organize their desktops so they can work more efficiently. Can you do it?" The three students stole quick glances at each other, knowing perfectly well that they had never used Microsoft Windows NT before, but ended up nodding politely. "Great! Take the morning to get prepared and we'll meet my CAD operators right after lunch. I'll see you later."

In this session, you and our three students will learn the advantages of using Microsoft Windows NT. You will also be able to describe its components, arrange windows on the screen, and access the Help system. This session provides the foundation for the remaining lessons in this guide.

WHAT IS WINDOWS NT?

Microsoft Windows NT[1] is an operating system. An **operating system** is a collection of software programs that manage, coordinate, and, in a sense, bring life to the computer hardware (the physical components of a computer). Every computer must have an operating system to control its basic input and output operations, such as receiving commands from the keyboard or mouse (input) and displaying

---
[1]NT is an abbreviation for "New Technology."

information to the screen (output). An operating system is also responsible for managing the storage areas of the computer, namely hard disks and diskettes, and for connecting to networks and the Internet. Without an operating system, you cannot communicate with your computer.

THE WINDOWS ADVANTAGE

Microsoft Windows NT, like previous versions of Windows, provides a common graphical environment for working in your application software, such as Microsoft Word or Netscape Navigator. The knowledge you gain from learning one Windows program will help you to learn and become productive in other Windows programs. Some additional advantages of using Windows NT include these factors:

- The ability to run more than one application at a time with built-in preemptive **multitasking,** discussed further in later sessions.

- The ability to copy and move information within an application or among applications using the Clipboard program.

- The ability to share information by linking or embedding objects from one application into another using ActiveX and OLE technologies.

- The ability to display graphical elements on the screen as you will see them printed, including different fonts, colors, and images.

THE WINDOWS FAMILY

The Microsoft solution for desktop operating systems provides a suite of products sharing the same user interface and technologies. As of this writing, there are four operating systems available from Microsoft:

- WINDOWS CE   For people using small communications, entertainment, and mobile-computing devices. Windows CE provides a subset of Windows 95 functionality for users of Personal Digital Assistants (PDAs) and other sub-notebook devices.

- WINDOWS 95   For home and business desktop computer users, and for users of notebook computers or multimedia systems. This operating system is used by the majority of personal computer users and is preloaded on many retail computer systems.

- WINDOWS NT WORKSTATION   For business and power users requiring an industrial-strength and fault-tolerant operating system. NT Workstation is the premier operating system for high-end statistical applications, graphics, desktop video and animation, and Computer-Aided Drafting (CAD).

- WINDOWS NT SERVER   For networking applications in small to large enterprises that require high levels of reliability and security. With Microsoft BackOffice and the Internet Information Server (IIS), NT Server provides a host of complementary software solutions for accessing SQL databases and creating Web sites.

Both NT Workstation and NT Server are based on the same underlying architecture and have the same look and feel. However, NT Workstation is optimized for the desktop and NT Server is geared toward networking applications. This guide assumes that you are using the Workstation edition of Windows NT 4.0. For information on configuring a network using NT Server, we recommend studying the Microsoft NT Resource Kit.

WINDOWS 95 AND NT WORKSTATION

There are as many similarities between Windows 95 and Windows NT Workstation 4.0 as there are differences. While they share the same programming and user interfaces, the products' architectures differ substantially. Windows 95 is designed and marketed as a consumer operating system for the home and business. Windows NT Workstation is designed as an industrial-strength operating system for critical business applications that require high performance, connectivity, and security.

Table 1.1 provides a summary of the similarities and differences between Windows 95, Windows NT Workstation 4.0, and Windows NT Server 4.0.

TABLE 1.1	Feature	Windows 95	Windows NT Workstation 4.0	Windows NT Server 4.0
Operating System Comparison	Purpose of Operating System (OS) as stated by design goals	Consumer Desktop OS	Power-User Desktop OS	Enterprise Network OS
	Recommended minimum hardware configuration	486 8MB RAM	Pentium 16MB RAM	Pentium 32MB RAM
	Plug and Play technology for easy hardware installation	Yes	No	No
	Built-in features for reliability, stability, and security	Good	Excellent	Excellent
	Compatibility with 16-bit and 32-bit software applications	Excellent	Good	Good
	Number of processors (CPUs) supported by operating system	1	2	32

Windows NT is designed to be a more robust and secure operating system than Windows 95. Therefore, applications like DOS-based multimedia applications that need to communicate directly to hardware devices, such as sound cards, may not work properly under NT. Also, Windows NT does not support virtual device drivers that are required by some fax and remote control communication programs. On the other hand, if you require a robust and secure operating system with advanced networking features, Windows NT is the preferred choice over Windows 95.

If you are previewing this guide before deciding to upgrade from Windows 95 to Windows NT Workstation, consider the software applications you use and your current hardware configuration. You need to ensure that your applications will work with NT 4.0 and that your computer is powerful enough to take advantage of NT's advanced features. In revision updates slated for late 1997, Windows NT 4.0 may receive the Plug and Play, Advanced Power Management, and DirectX support that Windows 95 now enjoys.

WORKING WITH WINDOWS NT

One of the most important features of Windows NT is something that is completely hidden from your view. If you could take a peek "under the hood," you would find a true **32-bit operating system,** which means that Windows NT can work with 32 bits of data at one time—twice as much data as can be processed by any previous version of DOS (*D*isk *O*perating *S*ystem), which is a 16-bit operating system. What does a 32-bit design mean to you? Generally, individual Windows NT applications will run faster and you will be able to work with multiple applications at the same time without a noticeable delay. Also, you will be able to realize the full potential and power of your new Pentium™ computer!

Let's highlight some of the less concealed features of Windows NT.

THE WINDOWS NT METAPHOR

Like Windows 95, Windows NT 4.0 now refers to all the files you create using Windows applications as *documents*. You organize these files or documents into **folders.** Computer terms like "subdirectory" or "directory structure" are no longer used in Windows NT.

Another friendly aspect of Windows NT centers on the way it views documents. The old **application-specific approach,** which requires your focus to be on the application you use to create your work, has given way to the new **document-centric approach,** which lets you focus directly on the document or work that you must accomplish. In this sense, Windows NT works the way you work. For new computer users, this approach makes immediate sense. That is, in Windows NT you open a folder to display related documents, and then you open a document to view or edit its contents. Using this process, you never have to worry about opening the application—Windows NT takes care of that for you.

THE DESKTOP

The **desktop** (Figure 1.1) appears after you turn on your computer and load Windows NT. Think of the Windows desktop as your own desk in your home or office where you work with documents that reside in folders. Since the desktop represents your personal working area, it is likely that your Windows NT desktop will look slightly different from Figure 1.1.

FIGURE 1.1

THE WINDOWS NT
DESKTOP

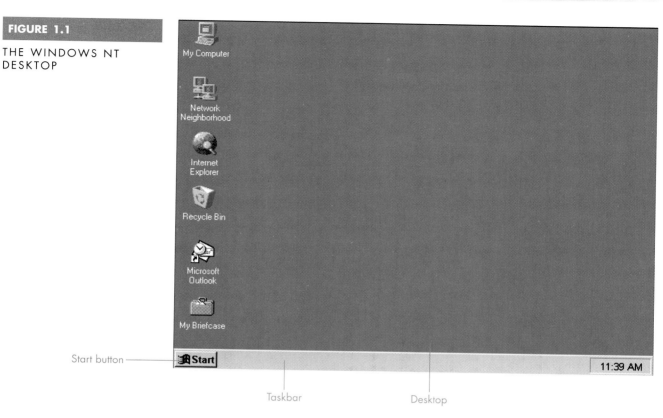

Start button

Taskbar   Desktop

In Windows NT, you open documents and applications in windows on the desktop. You can have multiple windows open at once, each displaying a different document or providing a different view of the same document. You use the mouse to size and move windows on the desktop and, thereby, organize your personal workspace.

We describe the desktop in more detail later in this session.

THE START BUTTON AND TASKBAR

Initially, the Start button (Start) is positioned on the taskbar and located in the bottom left-hand corner of the desktop. In Windows NT, you can use the Start button to open documents and load applications with only two mouse clicks (as demonstrated later in this guide.) In fact, you can access 99 percent of the functionality that a novice user needs right from this button. And the best part is that the Start button is always visible, even when you're working in an application!

You may notice that only the Start button appears on the taskbar in Figure 1.1. As you start additional applications, new buttons representing each open application will appear to the right of the Start button. To switch between applications (also called *tasks*), you simply click the desired button once on the taskbar. Multitasking in Windows NT 4.0 is as easy as changing channels on your television!

LONG FILENAMES

Previous users of DOS and early Windows software had to adhere to strict rules when naming files. A complete DOS filename consisted of a file name and an extension, separated by a period (for example, FILENAME.EXT). Every disk file required a name containing one to eight characters, with no spaces. The filename extension of up to three characters, however, was optional. The eight-character name of the file had to reflect its content, while the three-character extension commonly indicated the application software program used to create the file.

With Windows 95 and Windows NT 4.0, the shackles have been removed! You can now use up to 255 characters, including spaces, to descriptively name your files. Instead of "BUDGET97.XLS," you can write "1997 Western Regional Budget." Most of the documents you create in newer applications can also store file properties, such as keywords, comments, and other information. These two features, long filenames and document properties, make searching for files in your disk storage areas much easier.

"MY COMPUTER" AND "NETWORK NEIGHBORHOOD"

The "My Computer" and "Network Neighborhood" icons enable you to easily see what's in your computer and to scan your network connections. These two applications make extensive use of windows and **icons,** which are pictures or symbols, to represent everything from hardware devices to file folders. You launch the "My Computer" and "Network Neighborhood" applications by double-clicking their desktop icons using the mouse.[2] If you want to see the files or documents on a diskette drive, for example, you double-click the "My Computer" icon ( ) to display your computer's resources and then double-click the icon representing your computer's diskette drive. A new window appears on the desktop displaying the files located on the drive.

NT EXPLORER

Like "My Computer" and "Network Neighborhood," the Windows NT Explorer helps you manage the folders, files, and disks on your computer or network. While "My Computer" and "Network Neighborhood" use icons and overlapping windows on the desktop, NT Explorer uses a single window with a dual-paned hierarchical view of your computer's resources. Those of you accustomed to the previous Windows File Manager will feel quite at home using NT Explorer. For experienced users, NT Explorer provides the most efficient means for managing your computer's contents and network connections.

WINDOWS MESSAGING CLIENT

If you have a modem in your computer or access to a network, the Windows Messaging service can be used to send and receive electronic mail messages and documents. The Windows Messaging software, previously known as the Exchange client, is also called the universal inbox because it provides a single place for you to receive your incoming communications, including Internet mail. Unfortunately,

---

[2]If your computer isn't connected to a network, you will only see the "My Computer" icon ( ) on the desktop.

the initial release of Windows NT does not let you send or receive faxes from the inbox. In Figure 1.1, the Inbox icon (🌐) has been replaced by the new Outlook (🕮) information manager that ships with Microsoft Office 97. If you have not installed Office 97, you may still have the Exchange Inbox on your desktop.

WINDOWS ACCESSORIES

Several accessory programs are included with Windows NT, ranging from network management and communications software to a full-featured word processing program. **Accessory programs** are often included in operating systems to support, enhance, and expand the utility of other application programs. Some of the accessory programs provided in Windows NT (and discussed in Session 2) include WordPad, Paint, HyperTerminal, Calculator, and Phone Dialer. NT 4.0 also provides the Internet Explorer web browser for use in surfing the World Wide Web.

WINDOWS NT AND THE INTERNET

Using Windows NT, you can easily access the Internet. For those of you new to the online world, the **Internet** is a vast collection of computer networks that spans the entire planet, made up of many smaller networks connected by standard telephone lines. The term **Intranet** refers to a local or wide area network that uses Internet technologies to share information within an organization. Many corporations are establishing Intranets using Windows NT to more easily disseminate information to their employees.

To access the Internet, you need a network or modem connection that links your computer to an account on the university or college's network or to an independent Internet Service Provider (ISP). Once connected, you use web browser software, such as Microsoft Internet Explorer (included with Windows NT), to access the **World Wide Web (WWW).** The WWW provides a visual interface for the Internet and lets you search for information by simply clicking on highlighted words and images, known as **hyperlinks.** When you click a link, you are telling your web browser to retrieve and then display a page from a web site. Each web page has a unique location or address specified by its *Uniform Resource Locator* or URL. One example of a URL is: http://www.microsoft.com. For more information on the Internet and World Wide Web, visit your local bookstore, campus computing center, or computer users group.

In addition to Internet Explorer, NT Workstation ships with Microsoft's Peer Web services (PWS) software and NT Server includes the Internet Information Server (IIS) software. For small scale Intranets, the NT Workstation and PWS combination makes it easy to develop and publish personal Web pages in a peer-to-peer networking environment. The NT Workstation license even allows ten users to connect to and access your computer, which is sufficient for developing, testing, and implementing a small scale Intranet. Like the Internet Information Server, PWS supports all the Information Server Application Programming Interface (ISAPI) extensions. However, you need NT Server and the IIS software to fully implement a Web site that supports FTP, HTTP, and Gopher services.

As you proceed through this manual, look for the Internet integration features found in the *In Addition* boxes.

Starting Windows NT

This session assumes that you are working on a computer with Microsoft Windows NT Workstation 4.0 loaded on the hard disk drive. Before you load Windows, let's look at how to use the mouse and keyboard.

HOW THE MOUSE IS USED

Regardless of whether your mouse has two or three buttons, you use the left or primary mouse button for selecting menu commands and objects that appear on the desktop or within windows. You use the right mouse button to display shortcut menus for objects.

The most common mouse actions in Windows NT are:

- Point   Slide the mouse on your desk to position the tip of the mouse pointer over the desired object on the screen.

- Click   Press down and release the left mouse button quickly. Clicking is used to select icons, to position the cursor, and to select menu commands.

- Right-Click   Press down and release the right mouse button quickly. Right-clicking the mouse pointer on an object, such as an icon, displays a context-sensitive shortcut menu, if available.

- Double-Click   Press down and release the mouse button twice in rapid succession. Double-clicking is used in Windows to select and open an object, such as the "My Computer" icon (🖳) on the desktop.

- Drag   Press down and hold the mouse button as you move the mouse pointer across the screen. When the mouse pointer reaches the desired location, release the mouse button. Dragging is used to move objects or windows and to create shortcuts for objects.

You may notice that the mouse pointer changes shape as you move it over different parts of the screen or when an application performs a certain task. Each mouse pointer shape has its own purpose and may provide you with important information. There are four primary mouse pointer shapes you should be aware of:

       left arrow   Used to select objects, choose menu commands, and access buttons on the taskbar and application toolbars.

       hourglass   Informs you that Windows is occupied and requests that you wait.

I	I-beam	Used to edit text and to position the insertion point (also called a *cursor*).
	hand	In the Help window, the hand is used to select shortcuts and definitions.

Aside from being the primary input device for entering text, the keyboard offers shortcut methods for performing some common commands and procedures. In this learning guide, we describe keyboard procedures only when they provide the most efficient means for performing a task. Although this guide concentrates on the easiest methods, we recommend that you try the others and decide which you prefer. *Don't memorize all of the information in this guide! Be selective and find your favorite methods.*

Enough talk! Let's get to work.

LOADING WINDOWS NT

This session assumes that you are working on a computer that uses NT Workstation as its primary operating system. Because Windows NT is an operating system, it is loaded into the computer's memory when you first turn on the computer. Although the OS Loader menu may appear when the computer is first turned on, you can usually ignore the menu choices to load the default NT Workstation configuration.

Perform the following steps . . .

1. Turn on the power switches to the computer and monitor. If the OS Loader menu appears, use the cursor keys to highlight "Windows NT Workstation Version 4.00" from the menu and then press **(ENTER)**. After a few seconds, the initial Windows Logon screen is displayed.

2. PRESS: **(CTRL)** + **(ALT)** + **(DELETE)** at the Begin Logon window

3. In the Logon Information dialog box that appears, you must enter your user name and password. If you do not know this information, please ask your instructor or lab assistant. Then, do the following:
   SELECT: *User name* text box
   TYPE: *your user name*
   SELECT: *Password* text box
   TYPE: *your password*
   (*Hint*: You select a text box by moving the mouse pointer over the box and clicking the left mouse button once. To select the text within a text box, drag the I-beam mouse pointer over the text. When you begin typing, the highlighted text will be replaced.)

4. Unless the feature has been disabled, a Welcome dialog box appears with a usability tip (shown in Figure 1.2) each time you load Windows. You can easily disable this feature by deselecting the check box in the lower-left corner of the dialog box. However, these tips provide a useful reminder of features that you may be underutilizing. If the Welcome dialog box appears

on your screen, leave the check box selected and then do the following:
CLICK: Close command button

FIGURE 1.2

WELCOME SCREEN

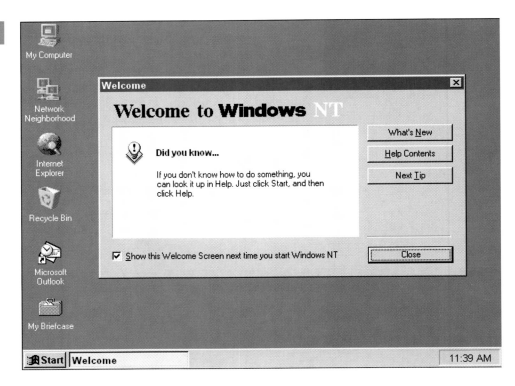

5. If additional windows appear open on your desktop:
CLICK: Close button ([×]) in the top right-hand corner of each open window

---

QUICK REFERENCE
Loading NT
Workstation

1. **Turn on your computer.**
2. **Select "Windows NT Workstation Version 4.0" from the OS Loader menu and then press** (ENTER).
3. **PRESS:** (CTRL) + (ALT) + (DELETE) **at the Begin Logon window**
4. **In the appropriate text box of the Logon Information dialog box:**
    TYPE: your user name and password
5. **PRESS:** (ENTER)

IN ADDITION REDISPLAYING THE WELCOME TO WINDOWS NT SCREEN

If you've previously disabled the Welcome to Windows NT dialog box and want to display it again each time your computer starts, choose the Help command from the Start button ([Start]). In the Help dialog box, select the Tips and Tricks topic, the Tips of the Day topic, and then the Viewing the Welcome screen option. Follow the instructions for displaying the Welcome screen. Close the Help window by clicking its Close button ([×]).

EXECUTING TASKS

Performing a *task* in Windows refers to starting a program, executing a command, opening a data file, or customizing the desktop. In the following section, you practice using the Start button to execute tasks.

 **THE START BUTTON**

The Start button provides the easiest method for new users to execute a variety of tasks. The following exercise shows you how to launch applications from the Start menu.

 **Perform the following steps . . .**

1. CLICK:
   The Start menu pops upwards from the button. Notice that a right-pointing arrowhead appears next to some of the menu commands. An arrowhead indicates that a cascading menu will display if you position the mouse pointer on the option. In other words, you do not have to click the mouse button to display a command's cascading menu.

2. Using the mouse pointer, point to the Programs command. A menu should cascade from the Programs command and display to the right of the Start menu. Your screen may appear similar, but not identical, to Figure 1.3.

FIGURE 1.3

START, PROGRAMS
CASCADING MENU

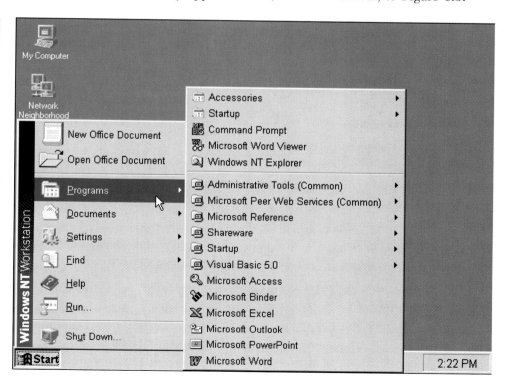

3. With the mouse pointer on the Programs command, slide the pointer to the right until you see a highlight appear in the Program cascading menu. You can now move the menu highlight up and down the list using the mouse pointer. Notice that you don't have to click the menu option to display its cascading menu. Point to the Accessories command to display another cascading menu.

4. Point to the Settings command on the Start menu. The Settings cascading menu now replaces the menus that were previously displayed.

5. To leave the menu:
   CLICK: *on a blank area of the desktop*

6. Now let's open a window on the desktop:
   CLICK: [Start]

7. CHOOSE: Settings
   This instruction tells you to position and hold the mouse pointer over the Settings command.

8. To open the Control Panel window:
   CHOOSE: Control Panel
   (*Note:* To execute the command, you need to click the left mouse button when the highlight appears on the Control Panel option.) The Control Panel window appears on the desktop.

9. With the Control Panel window visible, continue to the next section to learn more about the elements that are common to all windows.

QUICK REFERENCE	
QUICK REFERENCE Accessing Commands Using the Start Button	1. **CLICK:** [Start] 2. **CHOOSE:** *a menu command* **by clicking it or by pointing to it** 3. **To leave the menu without making a selection:** **CLICK: a blank area anywhere on the desktop**

ELEMENTS OF A WINDOW

If you completed the last section, the Control Panel window (Figure 1.4) should appear on the desktop. Our objective right now isn't to describe the purpose of the Control Panel; we'll save that discussion for later in this guide. This section familiarizes you with the common characteristics or elements of a window.

➧ TITLE BAR   The Title bar, located at the top of a window, contains the name of the application, current topic, or current document. In Figure 1.4, "Control Panel" appears in the Title bar. The Title bar also differentiates an active window, which typically has a darker-colored Title bar, from an inactive window. The **active window** is the window in which you are currently working. Using the mouse, you can move a window by dragging its Title bar.

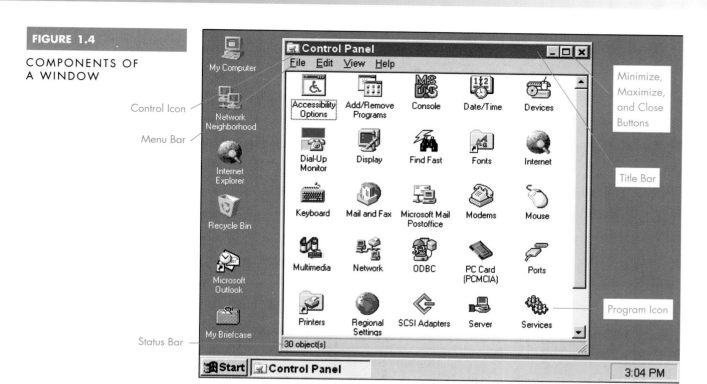

FIGURE 1.4

COMPONENTS OF
A WINDOW

- MENU BAR   The Menu bar appears immediately below the Title bar and contains commands for manipulating information in the window. The Menu bar is accessed by clicking on a desired command using the mouse. When activated, the Menu bar displays a pull-down menu. (*Note*: Not all windows have a Menu bar.)

- CONTROL ICON   Every window has a Control icon[3] that appears in the top left-hand corner of the window. If you click the icon, a Control menu appears that you can use to manipulate the window using the keyboard. Since it is easier to manipulate windows using a mouse, you will not spend much time accessing these commands. You can also close a window by double-clicking its Control icon.

- MINIMIZE, MAXIMIZE, AND RESTORE BUTTONS   The Minimize and Maximize buttons are located in the top right-hand corner of a window. You click the Minimize button (▬) to minimize a window from view when it is not currently needed but must remain running. By clicking the Maximize button (▢), you enlarge the window to fill the entire screen. When a window is maximized, the Restore button (▤) appears in its place. With the Restore button, you can return a window to its original size. (*Note*: A Restore button does not appear in Figure 1.4.)

- CLOSE BUTTON   You use the Close button (✖) in the top right-hand corner of a window to close the window with a single mouse click. When you close a window, you also remove its name from the taskbar.

---

[3]The picture used for the Control icon changes depending on the window type.

- STATUS BAR   The Status bar provides useful information about the window. For example, the Control Panel's Status bar tells you how many objects appear in the window. When you access a window's Menu bar, a helpful description of the selected command often appears in the Status bar. Whether minimized or maximized, a window has an associated button with its name and icon appearing on the taskbar.

- SCROLL BARS   When there is more information than can fit in a window at a single time, scroll bars are displayed at the right and/or bottom borders. You use the scroll bars to move around in a window by clicking the arrow heads (◄, ►, ▲, ▼) at either end of the scroll bar or by dragging the scroll box (☐) that is located on the scroll bar.

MENU BAR

Commands are grouped together on the Menu bar, located below the Title bar. To execute a command, you first select a menu option and then choose a command from its pull-down menu. Any commands on a pull-down menu that are not available for selection appear dimmed (usually a light gray in color). A check mark beside a command means that the command is currently active or that the feature is enabled.

To access the Menu bar using the mouse, position the mouse pointer on the desired menu option and click once to display the pull-down menu. You then click the mouse pointer on the command you want to execute.

Let's quickly practice accessing the Menu bar and choosing commands.

 **Perform the following steps . . .**

1. Ensure that the Control Panel window remains open on the desktop.

2. To browse the pull-down menus, position the mouse pointer over the File option in the Menu bar.

3. CLICK: left mouse button
   The File pull-down menu appears.

4. Using the mouse, point to the other options on the Menu bar. As you move the mouse pointer over an option, its pull-down menu appears.

5. To leave the Menu bar without selecting a command, point to a blank area on the Title bar and then click the left mouse button once. The highlight in the Menu bar disappears.

6. To execute a command from the Menu bar, do the following:
   CHOOSE: Help, About Windows NT
   This command tells you to click on the Help option in the Menu bar and then to select the About Windows NT command that appears in the pull-down menu. You should now see the About Windows NT window (Figure 1.5.)

FIGURE 1.5

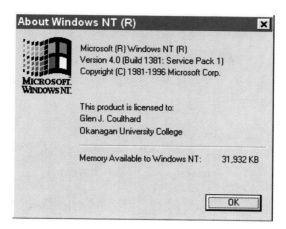

7. To close the About Windows NT window:
   CLICK: OK command button
   You can close this window by clicking the OK command button or by clicking its Close button ([×]).

8. To close the Control Panel window:
   CLICK: its Close button ([×])
   Notice that the Control Panel button also disappears from the taskbar.

QUICK REFERENCE
Using a Window's
Menu Bar

1. **CHOOSE: a menu option by clicking it with the mouse**

2. **CHOOSE: a menu command from its pull-down menu by clicking it
   with the mouse**

DIALOG BOX

A dialog box (Figure 1.6) is a common element in Windows applications that is used to collect information before processing a command or instruction. Dialog boxes are also used to display messages or to ask for the confirmation of commands. In a dialog box, you enter text and select options. Dialog boxes are sometimes composed of multiple tabs that allow you to access additional pages within the dialog box by simply clicking on the named tab. The three tabs displayed in Figure 1.6 are *General*, *Tools*, and *Sharing*. When you are finished making selections, click the OK command button to proceed.

FIGURE 1.6

A DIALOG BOX

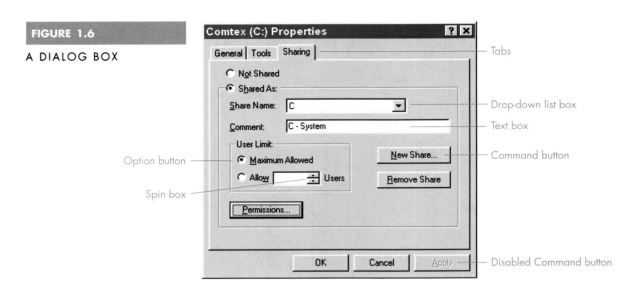

A dialog box uses several types of controls or components for collecting information. We describe the most common components in Table 1.2.

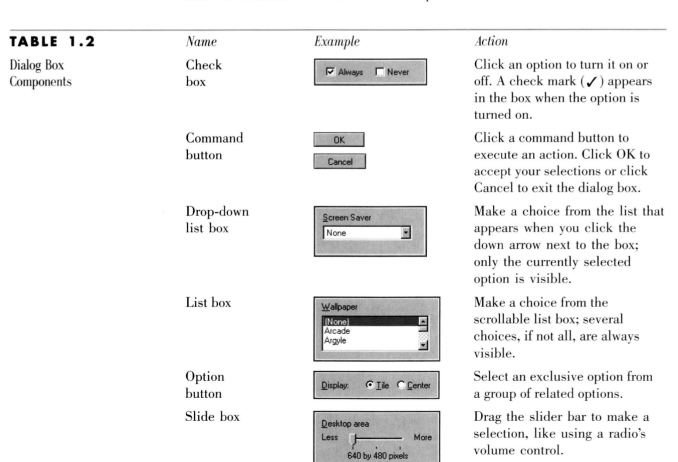

TABLE 1.2	*Name*	*Example*	*Action*
Dialog Box Components	Check box	☑ Always ☐ Never	Click an option to turn it on or off. A check mark (✓) appears in the box when the option is turned on.
	Command button	OK Cancel	Click a command button to execute an action. Click OK to accept your selections or click Cancel to exit the dialog box.
	Drop-down list box	Screen Saver None	Make a choice from the list that appears when you click the down arrow next to the box; only the currently selected option is visible.
	List box	Wallpaper (None) Arcade Argyle	Make a choice from the scrollable list box; several choices, if not all, are always visible.
	Option button	Display: ● Tile ○ Center	Select an exclusive option from a group of related options.
	Slide box	Desktop area Less ▬▬ More 640 by 480 pixels	Drag the slider bar to make a selection, like using a radio's volume control.

	Name	Example	Action
TABLE 1.2 **Continued**	Spin box	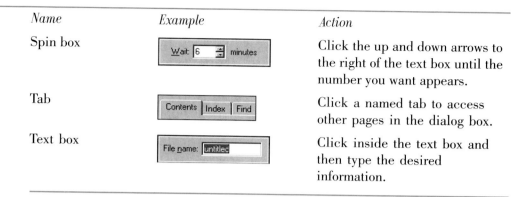	Click the up and down arrows to the right of the text box until the number you want appears.
	Tab		Click a named tab to access other pages in the dialog box.
	Text box		Click inside the text box and then type the desired information.

Most dialog boxes also provide a question mark button (**?**) beside the Close button (**✗**) on the Title bar. If you ever have a question about an element in a dialog box, click the question mark (**?**) and then click the component you want help with to display a pop-up help window. To remove the help window, click on it once.

SWITCHING TASKS

Before selecting a command from a window's Menu bar, you should first make the window active by selecting it using the mouse or taskbar. You switch between tasks, or windows, by clicking on a window's Title bar or on its name on the taskbar. Using the taskbar to switch among tasks is known as *push-button task switching* because, with a push or single click of a button, you can switch to a different task.

In this exercise, you launch two of the accessory programs that ship with Windows NT and then practice switching between them using the mouse.

Perform the following steps . . .

1. To start the Notepad accessory:
   START: Programs, Accessories, Notepad
   The Notepad window should appear on the desktop.

2. With the Notepad accessory remaining open, let's now launch a game of Solitaire:
   START: Programs, Accessories, Games, Solitaire
   You should now see two open application windows on your desktop, unless the Solitaire window is covering up the Notepad window. You will also see two buttons, representing the two applications, on the taskbar next to the Start button. You can easily determine that the Solitaire window is active because its Title bar is darker in color and its button on the taskbar appears depressed or pushed in.

3. To make the Notepad's application window active:
   CLICK: Notepad button on the taskbar
   The "Untitled - Notepad" window now appears in the foreground, overlaying the Solitaire window.

4. To switch to the Solitaire window by clicking its Title bar, move the Notepad window downwards by dragging its Title bar until you can see the Solitaire window's Title bar. If you can already see the Solitaire window's Title bar, proceed to the next step.

5. To make the Solitaire window active:
CLICK: Title bar of the Solitaire window

6. With the Notepad and Solitaire windows open on the desktop, continue to the next section to practice manipulating windows and icons.

Both of the above methods for switching between windows and tasks are useful. When working with more than one window on the desktop, a window's Title bar can easily become hidden from view. In this case, you can use the taskbar to switch to the hidden window.

QUICK REFERENCE
Switching Between
Windows

- **CLICK: a window's Title bar on the desktop, or**
- **CLICK: a window's button on the taskbar**

IN ADDITION WINDOWS NT TASK MANAGER

Windows NT provides you with the Task Manager for even greater control over open applications. In addition to letting you close errant windows that do not respond t

mouse clicks, you can use Task Manager to monitor and evaluate your system's performance. We discuss Task Manager in more detail at the end of Session 2.

MANIPULATING WINDOWS AND ICONS

In this section, you practice using the buttons that are common to all windows, such as the Minimize and Maximize buttons. You also learn how to size, move, and organize windows. Similar to shuffling pages on your desk, you manipulate application windows on the Windows desktop so that you can work more efficiently.

MINIMIZING AND MAXIMIZING A WINDOW

Let's practice using the Minimize (▬) and Maximize (▢) buttons on a window's Title bar. You will also use the Restore button (▣) to return a window to its original size. These buttons provide single-click functionality for manipulating windows.

Perform the following steps . . .

1. Ensure that the Notepad and Solitaire windows are open on the desktop.

2. To make the Notepad window the active window:
   CLICK: Notepad button on the taskbar

3. To maximize the Notepad window to fill the entire screen:
   CLICK: Maximize button (□) on its Title bar
   Notice that the maximized window does not cover the taskbar.

4. To restore the window to its original size:
   CLICK: Restore button (🗗)

5. To minimize the Notepad window:
   CLICK: Minimize button (▬)
   Although buttons for both windows appear on the taskbar, only the Solitaire window is open on the desktop. Because the Solitaire window is now active, its button on the taskbar appears pushed in.

6. To minimize the Solitaire window:
   CLICK: Minimize button (▬) on its Title bar

7. To display the Notepad window again:
   CLICK: Notepad button on the taskbar
   (*Note:* You do not have to double-click the button on the taskbar.)

8. Continue to the next section to practice closing windows.

QUICK REFERENCE
Minimizing and
Maximizing Windows

- CLICK: Maximize button (□) to maximize a window
- CLICK: Restore button (🗗) to restore a maximized window to its original size
- CLICK: Minimize button (▬) to minimize the window, but keep it available for use

CLOSING A WINDOW

The easiest method for closing a window is to click its Close button (✕). However, you can also use the taskbar and Control icon to manipulate windows that are open on the desktop. Let's practice the most common of these methods now.

 Perform the following steps . . .

1. To close the Notepad window using the Close button:
   CLICK: Close button (✕) on its Title bar
   The Notepad button no longer appears on the taskbar.

2. To close the Solitaire window using the taskbar's shortcut menu:
   RIGHT-CLICK: Solitaire button on the taskbar
   CHOOSE: Close from the shortcut menu
   There are now no open windows displayed on the desktop.

- **CLICK: a window's Close button (☒), or**
- **DOUBLE-CLICK: a window's Control icon, or**
- **RIGHT-CLICK: a window's button on the taskbar**
  CHOOSE: Close

MOVING A WINDOW

You move a window by dragging its Title bar using the mouse. In this exercise, you practice using the mouse to position windows on your desktop.

Perform the following steps . . .

1. Let's open a new window to work with in this section:
   START: Settings, Control Panel
   The Control Panel window appears on the desktop.

2. Position the mouse pointer on the Control Panel's Title bar.

3. To move the window:
   CLICK: the left mouse button and hold it down
   DRAG: the window to the bottom-right corner of the screen
   Notice that a shadow of the window frame moves as you drag the mouse. (*Note:* Depending on your default display options, the entire window, and not just a frame, may move when you drag the Title bar.)

4. When you are satisfied that the window is positioned correctly, release the mouse button to complete the move operation.

5. Now move the Control Panel window to the top left-hand corner of the screen.

6. With the Control Panel window open on the desktop, continue to the next section.

1. **Position the mouse pointer on the window's Title bar.**
2. **CLICK: the left mouse button and hold it down**
3. **DRAG: the window frame to a new location**
4. **Release the left mouse button to complete the move operation.**

SIZING A WINDOW

You size a window by dragging its borders using the mouse. You can also drag the enlarged sizing corner (shown below) in the bottom right-hand corner of a window frame to size it both horizontally and vertically. In most applications, changing the size of a window does not affect the contents of the window.

Sizing Corner

You practice sizing the Control Panel window in this exercise.

Perform the following steps . . .

1. Ensure that the Control Panel window appears in the top left-hand corner of the desktop.

2. To increase the width of the Control Panel window, first position the mouse pointer over the right vertical border. The mouse pointer changes to a black double-headed arrow when positioned correctly.

3. CLICK: the left mouse button and hold it down
   DRAG: mouse pointer to the right approximately 1 inch
   You will notice that a shadow of the border frame is moved with the mouse pointer. (*Note*: Depending on your default display options, the entire window, and not just a frame, is affected when you drag its border frame.)

4. To decrease the width of the Control Panel window, position the mouse pointer over the right vertical border until the pointer changes shape.

5. CLICK: the left mouse button and hold it down
   DRAG: mouse pointer to the left until the window contains two columns of icons
   Your screen should now look similar to Figure 1.7; however, the height of the window may be different.

FIGURE 1.7

SIZING A WINDOW

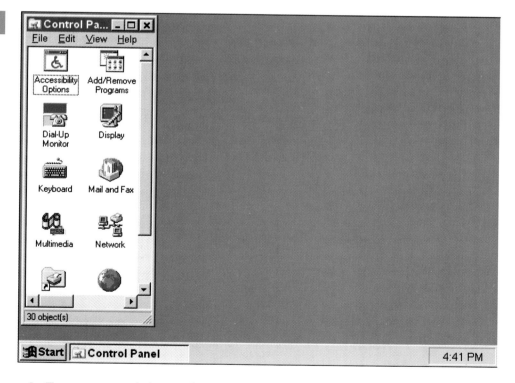

6. To move around the window:
   CLICK: arrows at the top and bottom of the vertical scroll bar

7. To move around the window using the vertical scroll box, first position the mouse pointer on the scroll box. (*Note:* Although we refer to a scroll box (▢) being a small box on the scroll bar, Windows NT provides proportionally-sized scroll boxes. For example, the size of a scroll box is determined by comparing the proportion of the window that is visible to the total window's size. In Figure 1.7, the scroll box is a long vertically-shaped bar, since most of the window is visible.)

8. CLICK: the left mouse button and hold it down
   DRAG: mouse pointer and scroll box along the scroll bar

9. To increase both the horizontal and vertical size of the Control Panel window, point to the bottom right-hand corner of the window until a diagonal, double-headed arrow appears.

10. CLICK: the left mouse button and hold it down
    DRAG: mouse pointer to the right and down until the window covers approximately two-thirds of the desktop, as shown in Figure 1.4
    When you release the mouse button, you should notice that the horizontal scroll bar disappears.

QUICK REFERENCE
Sizing a Window

1. **Position the mouse pointer on the window's border or corner until the mouse pointer changes to a double-headed arrow.**
2. **CLICK: the left mouse button and hold it down**
3. **DRAG: the window frame to increase or decrease its size**
4. **Release the left mouse button to complete the sizing operation.**

ARRANGING ICONS

After changing the size of a window, you may want to reorganize the displayed icons. The quickest method for arranging icons is to access a shortcut menu by right-clicking on an empty area in the window. There are two commands, Arrange Icons and Line up Icons, that enable you to rearrange icons in the active window. You can also choose the View command from the window's Menu bar to access these commands.

Even if the contents of your Control Panel window appear organized, do the following exercise to practice arranging icons.

Perform the following steps . . .

1. Position the mouse pointer on an empty area in the Control Panel window.

2. To access a shortcut menu for the window:
   RIGHT-CLICK: the mouse on the empty area

3. Point the mouse at the Arrange Icons command. The shortcut and cascading menu in Figure 1.8 should now appear. (*Note:* If the mouse pointer is positioned over an icon by accident, a different shortcut menu will appear.)

FIGURE 1.8

DISPLAYING A
WINDOW'S SHORTCUT
MENU

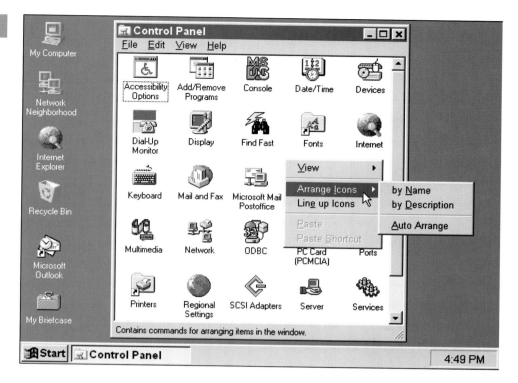

4. To have Windows manage the organization of icons in the window, you must choose the Arrange Icons, Auto Arrange command. If a check mark appears next to the Auto Arrange command, position the mouse pointer over an empty area of the window and click the left mouse button once to remove the shortcut menu. Otherwise, do the following to arrange the icons:
CHOOSE: Auto Arrange
By selecting the Auto Arrange command, Windows will automatically rearrange the icons whenever you size and display the window.

<table>
<tr><td>QUICK REFERENCE
Arranging Icons</td><td>● RIGHT-CLICK: an empty area in a window to display its shortcut menu

● CHOOSE: Arrange Icons or Line up Icons</td></tr>
</table>

IN ADDITION CHANGING THE WAY FILES AND ICONS ARE REPRESENTED

● To change the way items look in a window using the shortcut menu:
RIGHT-CLICK: *an empty area* in a window
CHOOSE: View command

CHOOSE: Large Icons, Small Icons, List, or Details

● To change the way items look in a window using the Menu bar:
CHOOSE: View from the menu
CHOOSE: Large Icons, Small Icons, List, or Details

ORGANIZING WINDOWS

In addition to moving windows manually, you can have Windows arrange all of your open windows in one step. To do so, you simply point to a blank spot on the taskbar and right-click with the mouse. The following menu will appear:

To layer the open windows on your desktop like a fanned deck of cards (Figure 1.9), you choose Cascade Windows from the shortcut menu. The active window is displayed on top of the other windows. To display the open windows in a floor tile pattern (Figure 1.10), you choose the Tile Windows Horizontally or Tile Windows Vertically commands. These commands do not affect windows that have been minimized to the taskbar.

In this section, you open the Solitaire, Paint, and Notepad accessory programs and then practice organizing their windows on the desktop.

Perform the following steps . . .

1. Ensure that the Control Panel window is open on the desktop.

2. Let's open some additional windows:
   START: Programs, Accessories, Games, Solitaire
   START: Programs, Accessories, Paint
   START: Programs, Accessories, Notepad

3. To display the taskbar's shortcut menu, you must right-click an empty part of the taskbar. However, the buttons on the taskbar may be covering all or most of the blank space. Therefore, we will increase the size of the taskbar. To begin, position the mouse pointer on the top edge of the taskbar until a double-headed arrow appears. Then, do the following:
   CLICK: the left mouse button and hold it down
   DRAG: the mouse pointer up until a taskbar frame appears

4. Release the left mouse button.
   The taskbar should now appear large enough for two rows of buttons.

5. RIGHT-CLICK: a blank area on the taskbar
CHOOSE: Cascade Windows command
Your desktop should now look similar to Figure 1.9.

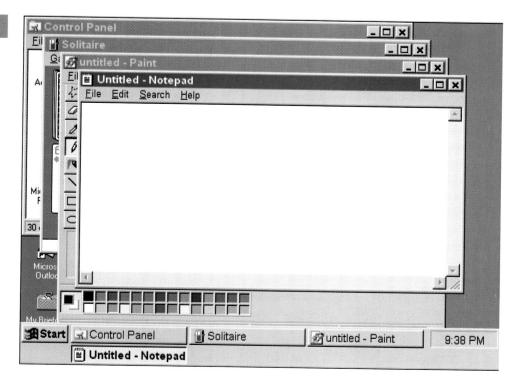

6. To tile the open windows:
RIGHT-CLICK: a blank area on the taskbar
CHOOSE: Tile Windows Horizontally
Your desktop should now look like Figure 1.10.

FIGURE 1.10

TILING OPEN WINDOWS

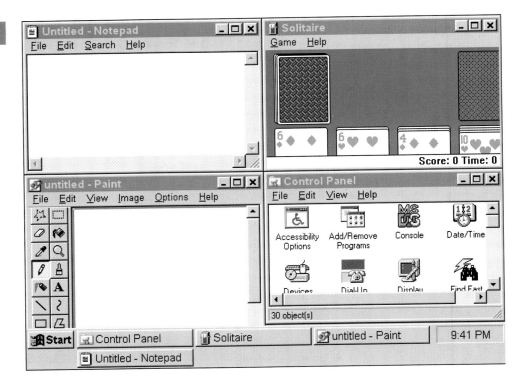

7. To minimize all open windows:
   RIGHT-CLICK: a blank area on the taskbar
   CHOOSE: Minimize All Windows

8. To undo the previous step:
   RIGHT-CLICK: a blank area on the taskbar
   CHOOSE: Undo Minimize All
   The windows should again appear in a tiled format.

9. Close each of the open windows by clicking its Close button (☒).

10. To return the taskbar to its original size, point to its top edge until a double-headed arrow appears. Then, do the following:
    CLICK: the left mouse button and hold it down
    DRAG: the mouse pointer down until a taskbar frame appears

11. Release the left mouse button.
    The taskbar is now returned to its original size. This is a useful method for temporarily removing the taskbar from view by dragging it down to the very bottom of the screen.

QUICK REFERENCE
Organizing Windows
on the Desktop

To arrange open windows on the desktop:
1. **RIGHT-CLICK: a blank area on the taskbar**
2. **CHOOSE: Cascade Windows, Tile Windows Horizontally, or Tile Windows Vertically from the shortcut menu**

QUICK REFERENCE
Resizing the Taskbar

1. **Position the mouse pointer on the taskbar's upper border until the mouse pointer changes to a double-headed arrow.**
2. **CLICK: the left mouse button and hold it down**
3. **DRAG: the window frame to increase or decrease its size**
4. **Release the left mouse button to complete the sizing operation.**

IN ADDITION MOVING THE TASKBAR

To move the taskbar, you can drag it to any edge of the screen. Point to an empty area on the taskbar and hold down the left mouse button while dragging the mouse pointer to an edge of the screen. A taskbar outline appears to help you guide the taskbar to its new location. Release the mouse button to complete the operation.

GETTING HELP

Windows NT Workstation provides several context-sensitive help features and a comprehensive library of online documentation. Like many developers trying to minimize the retail price of software and maximize profits, Microsoft has stopped shipping volumes of print-based documentation in favor of online and web-based Help options. This section describes the NT Workstation help features and how to find more detailed information.

CONTEXT-SENSITIVE HELP

Context-sensitive help refers to a program's ability to present helpful information reflecting your current position in the program. In Windows, you can often retrieve context-sensitive help for menu options, toolbar buttons, and dialog box items. The help information is presented concisely in a small pop-up window that you can remove with the click of the mouse. This type of help lets you access information quickly and then continue working without interruption. Table 1.3 describes some methods for accessing context-sensitive help while working in Windows.

TABLE 1.3	*To display...*	*Do this...*
Displaying context-sensitive help information	A description of a dialog box item	Click the question mark button ([**?**]) in a dialog box's Title bar and then click an item in the dialog box. Alternatively, you can often right-click a dialog box item and then choose the What's This? command from the shortcut menu.
	A description of a menu command	Choose the Help, What's This? command from the menu and then choose a command using the question mark mouse pointer. Rather than executing the command, a helpful description of the command appears in a pop-up window.
	A description of a toolbar button	Point to a toolbar button to display a pop-up label called a ToolTip.

In the following exercise, you will access context-sensitive help for an item in a dialog box.

Perform the following steps . . .

1. Ensure that there are no open windows on your desktop.

2. To display a dialog box for customizing the taskbar:
   RIGHT-CLICK: a blank area on the taskbar
   CHOOSE: Properties

3. For help on a particular item in the dialog box:
   CLICK: question mark button ([**?**])
   Your mouse pointer should now look like an arrow with a question mark attached.

4. To demonstrate context-sensitive help using this mouse pointer:
   CLICK: *Auto hide* check box
   A pop-up help window appears with a complete description of the check box option. Your screen should appear similar to Figure 1.11.

FIGURE 1.11

POP-UP HELP WINDOW
IN A DIALOG BOX

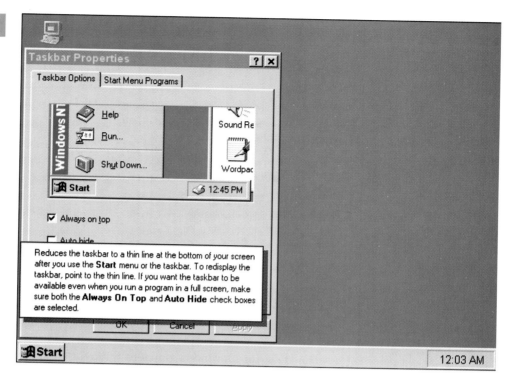

5. CLICK: the pop-up window once to remove it

6. To display help for another item in the dialog box:
   RIGHT-CLICK: *Always on top* check box
   Make sure that you click the right mouse button; otherwise, you make a selection in the dialog box.

7. CHOOSE: What's This? menu command
   A pop-up help window appears with a new description for this item.

8. CLICK: the pop-up window once to remove it

9. To remove the Taskbar Properties window:
   CLICK: its Close button (☒)

QUICK REFERENCE Displaying Context-Sensitive Help in a Dialog Box.	**1. CLICK: question mark button (?)** **2. Using the question mark mouse pointer, select the desired item for which you want to display a help pop-up window**

HELP TOPICS WINDOW

For a complete topical listing of the Help system, choose the Help command from the Start menu. This command displays the Help Topics window, as shown in Figure 1.12. You can think of the Help Topics window as the front door to the vast help resources in Windows NT.

FIGURE 1.12

HELP TOPICS WINDOW:
CONTENTS TAB

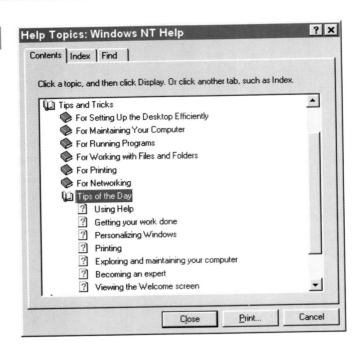

The Help Topics window provides three different tools, each on its own tab, to help you find the information you need quickly and easily. You point to and click a tab using the mouse to make the tab active in the window. Refer to the following tab descriptions to determine which tool you should use when requiring assistance:

- *Contents* tab

  This tab is your Table of Contents for the entire Help system. Notice in Figure 1.12 that there are three different types of icons displayed:

  - represents a help category; double-click a book icon to view the books and topics it contains
  - represents a displayed help category; double-click an open book icon to close (or collapse) the book
  - represents a help topic; double-click a topic icon to display a help window

- *Index* tab

  Displays an alphabetical list of keywords and phrases, similar to a traditional book index. To search for a topic using this tab, type a word (or even the first few letters of a word) into the text box.

- *Find* tab

  Provides the ability to conduct a full-text search of the Help system for finding a particular word or phrase. Although similar to the *Index* tab, this tab differs in its ability to look past indexed keywords and search the help text itself.

When you double-click a help topic, it is displayed in a *secondary* window. You may find that secondary windows include some unfamiliar buttons, like ⟩⟩ and ⬛, embedded in the help text. The ⟩⟩ symbol, which we'll call the Chiclet button, represents a "See Also" link or an "Execute" link that you can click to move to a related topic or run a program. The Show Me symbol (⬛) actually initiates the command you're interested in. You may also notice that some words or phrases in the help window have a dotted underline. If you click such a word or phrase, a definition pop-up window appears.

You will now access the Help Topics window.

Perform the following steps . . .

1. To display the Help Topics window:
   START: Help

2. CLICK: *Contents* tab
   (*Note*: The Help Topics window remembers the tab that was selected when it was last closed. It will automatically return to this tab the next time you access Help.)

3. To display the contents of a book:
   DOUBLE-CLICK: "📖 Tips and Tricks" book
   (*Note*: You can double-click the book icon (📖) or the book's title. If you find it difficult to double-click using the mouse, you can also select or highlight the book by clicking it once and then click the Open command button.)

4. To further clarify the search:
   DOUBLE-CLICK: "📖 Tips of the Day" book
   Your screen should now appear similar to Figure 1.12. Notice that this book contains multiple topics.

5. To display a help topic:
   DOUBLE-CLICK: "❓ Viewing the Welcome screen" topic
   The Help Topics window is removed from view and a secondary window appears with the topic information. Notice that this topic has a shortcut Show Me symbol (⬛).

6. After reading the help information, return to the Help Topics window:
   CLICK: Help Topics button under the Title bar

7. To access the Help Index:
   CLICK: *Index* tab

8. To retrieve help information on installing Windows NT:
   TYPE: installing
   Notice that the list box scrolls automatically to the first occurrence of the term. In this case, there are also several indented sub-categories to choose from.

9. DOUBLE-CLICK: "Components of Windows NT" help topic
   The Help Topics window disappears as a new secondary window is displayed with the help topic.

10. In order to print this topic for later reference:
    CLICK: Options button under the Title bar
    The following pop-up menu will appear.
    You can also display this menu by right-clicking in a help window.

<u>A</u>nnotate...
C<u>o</u>py
<u>P</u>rint Topic...
<u>F</u>ont ▶
<u>K</u>eep Help on Top ▶
<u>U</u>se System Colors

11. To remove the menu without making a selection, move the mouse pointer over a blank area on the desktop and then click the left mouse button once.

12. To close the Help window:
    CLICK: its Close button (☒)

QUICK REFERENCE
Searching for Help Using the Help Topics Window

1. **To display the Help Topics window:**

   START: Help

2. **CLICK:** *Contents* **tab to navigatge a hierarchical Help system**

   CLICK: *Index* **tab to search for a word or phrase in a keyword index**

   CLICK: *Find* **tab to conduct a full-text search of the Help system**

IN ADDITION ACCESSING HELP DIRECTLY FROM MICROSOFT

If you are connected to the Internet, you can keep current on product and company news by visiting Microsoft's web site. To access this site:

1. Establish an Internet connection.

2. Load the Microsoft Internet Explorer web browser software that is included with Microsoft NT, or launch the browser of your choice.

3. Point your browser to
   `http://www.microsoft.com`

Playing Games

Windows NT includes four games—FreeCell, Minesweeper, 3D Pinball, and Solitaire—for your enjoyment and to help you improve your mouse skills. We describe some of these games in the sections below. However, you may not have access to all of them on your computer system.

SOLITAIRE

Solitaire is a computer version of the popular card game. The objective of the game is to place the deck of 52 cards in four suit stacks at the top of the playing board. To do so, you first arrange the cards in descending order, using alternating colors (hearts or diamonds and spades or clubs). You build upon each of the original seven piles using cards from the other piles and the deck. To score points, you place cards in the suit stacks at the top of the screen in ascending order, starting with an Ace. When all cards appear in their respective suit stack, you have won the game. Figure 1.13 shows the Solitaire playing board in the middle of a game.

To load Solitaire, you choose Programs, Accessories, Games, Solitaire from the Start menu. To flip through the cards, you click the mouse pointer on the top card in the deck. To place a card in the suit stack, you double-click the card on the playing board or drag it to the desired stack. To arrange cards below a card pile on the playing board, you drag the card (or cards) using the mouse. To quit Solitaire, choose Game, Exit from the Menu bar.

FIGURE 1.13

THE SOLITAIRE
PLAYING BOARD

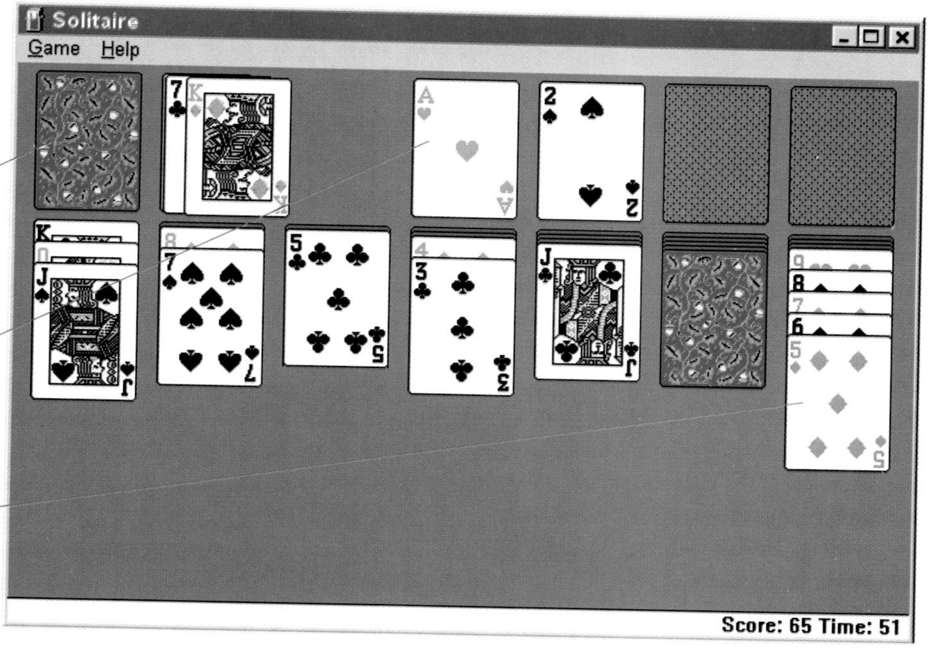

Click to view more
cards from the deck

Place cards from the same
suit in these four stacks

Build alternating suit colors in
these piles using drag and drop

PINBALL

Pinball (shown in Figure 1.14) is a game of both skill and chance. Although not included for its ability to teach mouse control, Microsoft does provide this game for two important reasons: entertainment and promotion. Obviously, the game is enjoyable to play but it is also an excellent demonstration of the graphics capabilities of Windows 95 and Windows NT.

FIGURE 1.14

STARTING 3D PINBALL

To start Pinball, you choose Programs, Accessories, Games, Pinball from the Start menu. The machine initially appears in a window but, for better performance, you should switch to Full Screen mode using the **F4** key or by choosing Options, Full Screen from the menu. To start the game, you depress the Plunger (Space Bar) and then control the flippers with the Z and / keys. To change these control options, choose Options, Player Controls from the menu. To quit Pinball, choose Game, Exit from the Menu bar.

EXITING WINDOWS NT

Windows refers to the task of exiting as "shutting down" the computer. You should always follow the suggested steps in this section before turning off the computer's power. Otherwise, you run the risk of losing your data. To exit Windows NT, you choose Start, Shut Down. The dialog box in Figure 1.15 appears.

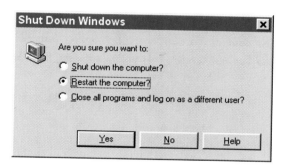

FIGURE 1.15

SHUT DOWN WINDOWS
DIALOG BOX

The option buttons in the Shut Down Windows dialog box are described in Table 1.4.

TABLE 1.4

Shut Down options

Command	When to Use
Shut down the computer?	Use this option when you are done with the current work session and want to turn off your computer.
Restart the computer?	Use this option when you want to continue working with Windows but you want to load a fresh copy of Windows NT into memory.
Close all programs and log on as a different user?	Use this option when your computer is connected to a network and you want to log on using a different User Name or prepare the computer for use by another person.

Windows remembers the layout of your desktop even after you turn your computer off. That is, if the "My Computer" window is displaying on the desktop when you shut down your computer, the window will reappear when you load Windows the next time. You will now shut down the computer to end the session.

Perform the following steps . . .

1. START: Shut Down
2. CLICK: *Shut down the computer?* option button
   CLICK: Yes or PRESS: [ENTER]

SUMMARY

Microsoft Windows NT is an operating system that enables you to interact with the computer using a Graphical User Interface (GUI). Besides controlling the input and output functions of the computer, an operating system provides the tools for file and disk management. This session introduced you to several features of Windows: the desktop and taskbar, My Computer, Network Neighborhood, NT Explorer, and Windows accessories,. In the latter half of the session, you loaded Microsoft Windows NT, executed tasks using the taskbar, and sized, moved, and arranged windows on the desktop. Finally, you learned how to access the Help system, practice mouse control with games, and how to exit Windows NT safely.

COMMAND SUMMARY

Many of the commands and procedures appearing in this session are provided in the command summary in Table 1.5.

TABLE 1.5

Command Summary

Task Description	General Instruction
Switch tasks or windows	Click the appropriate button name on the taskbar or click the window's Title bar.
Maximize, minimize, or restore a window	Click the Maximize button (□), Minimize button (_), or Restore button (◱).
Close a window	Click the Close (✗) button or right-click the button's name on the taskbar and choose Close.
Move a window	Drag the window by its Title bar to a new location.
Size a window	Drag a window's border or the sizing corner inward or outward.
Arrange icons	Right-click a blank area in a window and then choose the Arrange Icons or Line up Icons command.

TABLE 1.5
Continued

Task Description	General Instruction
Cascade windows	Right-click a blank area on the taskbar and then choose the Cascade Windows command.
Tile windows	Right-click a blank area on the taskbar and then choose the Tile Windows Horizontally or Tile Windows Vertically command.
Access help	START: Help
Launch games	START: Programs, Accessories, Games
Exit Windows NT	START: Shut Down CLICK: an option from the dialog box

KEY TERMS

32-bit operating system

An operating system that can work with and process data in 32-bit chunks, thereby increasing the speed of performing tasks.

accessory program

A program that is used to support, enhance, or expand existing programs in a computer system.

active window

The window that is currently selected; commands affect the active window only.

application-specific approach

With this approach to performing a task, the user must focus on the application instead of the document. *See document-centric approach.*

context-sensitive help

A Help feature that provides a concise description for a particular menu option, toolbar button, or dialog box item.

desktop

The principal interface between you and Windows NT. You start work from the desktop and organize your work on the desktop.

document-centric approach

With this approach to performing a task, the user can focus on the document instead of the application. This approach is generally more intuitive than the application-specific approach. *See application-specific approach.*

folder

In Windows, a folder is a tool for organizing files on a disk. Folders in Windows NT 4.0 are the same as *subdirectories* in Windows NT 3.51 or Windows 3.1.

hyperlinks

Text or graphics that when clicked take you to another resource location, either within the same document or to a separate document stored on your computer, a network server, an Intranet resource, or onto the Internet.

icons

Pictures or symbols that represent hardware, application programs, and data files.

Internet

A worldwide network of computer networks that are interconnected by standard telephone lines, fiber optics, and satellites.

Intranet

A local or wide area network that uses Internet protocols and technologies to share information within an institution or corporation.

multitasking

Activity in which more than one task or program is executed at a time. A small amount of each program is processed and then the CPU moves to the remaining programs, one at a time.

operating system

A collection of software programs that manage, coordinate, and control the computer hardware, input and output tasks, and storage system.

World Wide Web (WWW)

A visual interface to the Internet based on *hyperlinks*. Using web browser software, you click on hyperlinks to navigate the resources on the Internet.

EXERCISES

SHORT ANSWER

1. What is an operating system?

2. Describe three primary mouse movements in Windows.

3. Describe four common mouse pointer shapes.

4. How would you find out more information about a dialog box control?

5. Name the most common controls found in a dialog box.

6. What happens when you maximize a window?

7. What happens when you minimize a window?

8. What does it mean to *cascade* open windows?

9. Which of the Microsoft operating systems mentioned in this session would you recommend for a notebook computer? Why?

10. Which tab in the Help Topics window would you use first to search for help on "adding a CD-ROM" to your computer?

HANDS-ON

(*Note:* We assume that you have completed the material presented in this session. Also, ensure that the Advantage Diskette is placed into the diskette drive and then complete the following exercises in order.)

1. In this exercise, you practice opening and closing windows, switching between windows, and using a window's Menu bar.

    a. Start your computer to load Microsoft Windows NT.

    b. After logging on, close any windows that may already be open on the desktop.

    c. Perform the following tasks to open two windows:
        START: Programs, Accessories, Calculator
        START: Programs, Windows NT Explorer

    d. NT Explorer is the active window. Switch to the Calculator window. (*Hint:* Use either the Title bar or the taskbar to switch tasks.)

    e. Switch to NT Explorer.

    f. To practice using the Menu bar:
        CHOOSE: View, Large Icons
        CHOOSE: View, List
        CHOOSE: View, Details

    g. Close NT Explorer using the Close button.

    h. Close the Calculator accessory using the taskbar.

2. In this exercise, you maximize, minimize, cascade, and tile windows on the desktop.

    a. START: Programs, Windows NT Explorer
        START: Programs, Accessories, Games, Solitaire
        START: Settings, Printers
        START: Settings, Control Panel

    b. Minimize the Solitaire window.

    c. Maximize the Control Panel window.

    d. Restore the Control Panel window.

    e. Minimize all windows by right-clicking an empty area on the taskbar and then choosing Minimize All Windows. (*Note:* If necessary, increase the size of the taskbar.)

    f. Undo the previous step.

    g. Cascade all open windows.

    h. Tile all open windows horizontally.

    i. Close all open windows.

    j. If you changed the size of the taskbar, return it to its original size.

3. In this exercise, you practice moving and resizing windows on the desktop.

    a. START: Programs, Windows NT Explorer

    b. START: Programs, Accessories, Notepad

    c. START: Settings, Control Panel

    d. Cascade all open windows.

    e. Move and resize the windows on your desktop to resemble Figure 1.16.

    f. For each window, resize the window to take up about one-half of the desktop and then close it.

FIGURE 1.16

MOVING AND
SIZING WINDOWS

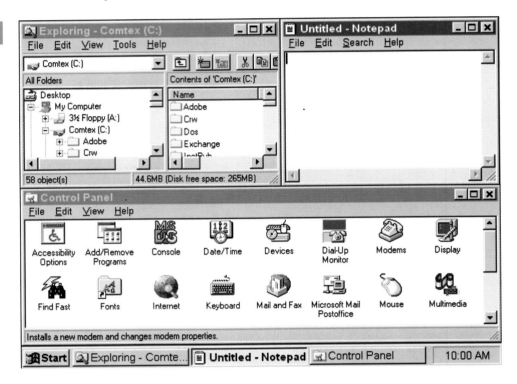

4. In this exercise, you practice arranging icons.

    a. DOUBLE-CLICK: "My Computer" icon (▣) on the desktop

    b. Resize the window to cover the top left quadrant of the screen.

    c. Right-click on an empty area inside the window to display its shortcut menu and arrange the icons in the window by Type.

    d. Arrange the icons in the window by Drive Letter.

    e. Auto-arrange the icons in the window.

    f. On your own, return the "My Computer" window to its original size.

    g. Close the "My Computer" window.

5. **On Your Own:** Explore a Microsoft Windows NT Help Topic
   Pick a Windows NT Help topic that interests you and write about it in a few paragraphs. Make sure to explain why you chose the topic and how to perform the procedures described. For example, you may be interested in learning how to connect your computer to the World Wide Web or how to customize the desktop. Use the Help Topics window for researching your topic.

6. **On Your Own:** Exploring Your Computer
   Using the mouse, display the right-click shortcut menu for the "My Computer" icon ( ) and then choose the Properties command. A dialog box with several tabs will appear. With the assistance of context-sensitive help, click the question mark button (**?**) and then explore the items and dialog box controls shown on these tabs. When you are finished exploring this dialog box, close it using the mouse.

CASE PROBLEMS   **CITY OF ALBERTVILLE, NEW YORK**

(*Note:* In the following case problems, assume the role of the primary characters and perform the same steps that they identify. You may want to reread the Case Study text at the beginning of this session.)

1. The three students sat quietly for the first few minutes after Buzz had left the meeting room. When they began to discuss how they were going to get prepared, Kyra offered the suggestion that they work through Session 1 of this guide. Having finished the session, they were now feeling much more confident with the task at hand. At 1:05 p.m., Buzz led the three students to meet the CAD operators. He fed them a few instructions as they walked down the narrow hallway. "This is an experienced group of draftspeople, but they know absolutely nothing about Microsoft Windows NT. To establish yourselves as knowledgeable computer users, I want you, Ralph, to explain to the group the significance of Windows' document-centric approach. Samantha, I want you to summarize the components of the Windows desktop, such as the Start button, taskbar and desktop icons. And Kyra, I want you to describe the advantages of using Windows. And try to provide examples related to their CAD work, if you can. Don't worry about specifics, they simply create letters using a word processor, budgets using spreadsheet software, and subdivision plans using the CAD graphics software. However, they do need to incorporate all these components into summary reports and Windows can surely help them perform that task. Well, we're here—are you ready?"

    For this exercise, prepare short speeches for Ralph, Samantha, and Kyra. You can either write the speeches by hand or use a computer, if you already know how. Make sure to use the most basic terms possible, but gear the presentations toward adult learners who are respected professionals in their own field.

2. After a successful presentation, Kyra is introduced to Samuel Weinhardt, the senior draftsperson for the department. Samuel is new to computers and works primarily as an inspector for computer-generated plans and reports. Although fascinated by the software, Samuel has had trouble mastering the mouse and has compiled a written list of problems that he now hands to Kyra. The list reads as follows:

   - *I've tried double-clicking on icons to move them, but I just seem to get windows opening up all over the place.*

   - *I don't understand the difference between an option button and a check box.*

   - *I've tried to size a window by clicking and holding down the right mouse button over its border, but it doesn't seem to work.*

   - *I've tried to move a window by clicking and holding down the left mouse button over its Maximize button, but it just expands the window.*

   - *The Cascade command doesn't seem to arrange the open windows in a floor tile pattern like it's supposed to.*

   - *I don't understand how an active window can be active when it's not moving.*

   - *My daughter told me to use the Solitaire game to practice my mouse skills, but I can't seem to find it.*

   Put yourself in Kyra's position and write down the answers, suggestions, and clarifications that you would give Samuel in response to his list.

3. Ralph and Samantha follow Janet Abdul's hand as she waves it across her computer screen, describing how she wants the desktop to look. "You know, what I really want is the Notepad, Calculator, and "My Computer" windows to display horizontally on the desktop like a layer cake. Also, I would like the game of Solitaire to be minimized so that I can access it whenever I need a break. Can you guys do that?"

   On your own computer, replicate what Janet Abdul wants her system to look like. Once finished, you need to provide written step-by-step instructions to Ralph and Samantha so that they will be able to make the changes on Janet's computer.

Microsoft Windows NT 4.0

Using WordPad and Other Accessories

SESSION

2

IRWIN

COMPUTER & INFORMATION TECHNOLOGY

INTRODUCTION

Most people use several tools to accomplish their daily work tasks. A landscaper uses a pick, shovel, and hoe to create a garden, while an accountant uses a columnar pad, pencil, and calculator to analyze a budget. The tools that you have available often determine your productivity in a job. How productive would the landscaper or accountant be without their shovel or calculator? Microsoft understands this correlation between tools and productivity, which is why they have included several accessory programs in the Windows NT package.

CASE STUDY	ADVANCED SOFTWARE DESIGN, INC.

Advanced Software Design, Inc. (ASD) is a software development company that specializes in writing Windows-based software applications. When requested, ASD submits proposals to companies and individuals who express a need for custom-written applications. For example, Harry Zidell of Business Assistance Services, an employment agency, recently contracted with ASD to build a skill-testing program for candidates. A few days after talking to Alethia Montera at ASD about his needs, Harry received a full proposal in the mail. The proposal looked fair, and the project is now underway.

While speaking to a client on the phone or in person, Alethia takes handwritten notes outlining the client's needs. After the conversation or meeting, she estimates the number of hours required to complete the project and calculates the cost of the job. She then sends her notes to Mary, who types them up and returns them to Alethia for final review. Alethia was recently given a computer by the programming department and has just started using Microsoft Windows. She wants to be able to use the programs that come bundled with Windows NT, like the word processor and calculator, to help her accomplish her work and to reduce the workload she places on Mary.

In this session, you and Alethia learn to use WordPad and Paint and are introduced to several other accessory programs. Lastly, you learn how to run multiple programs at the same time and how to share information among these programs. By the end of the session, you and Alethia will feel comfortable displaying the Accessories menu and experimenting with all the programs that are available in Windows NT Workstation.

WINDOWS NT ACCESSORIES

Although Windows NT is an operating system designed to manage your computer hardware, it provides you with a number of accessory programs, sometimes called *utilities*, designed to make you more productive. Windows' accessories can be categorized as follows:

- *General Applications.* Windows NT provides two writing tools: WordPad, a program for writing and formatting documents, and Notepad, a program for writing and editing text files. You can even enhance your documents using a drawing program called Paint.

- *Communications.* Extend the power of your computer using Windows NT communications utilities! For example, you can use the Microsoft Chat, Phone Dialer, and Telnet utilities, in addition to a full-featured communications program called HyperTerminal.

- *Multimedia.* **Multimedia** refers to technology that presents information using more than one medium, including text, graphics, animation, video, music, and narration. Windows includes a few multimedia accessories including CD Player, which is used for playing compact discs (CDs), and Media Player, which is used to play multimedia files. The Sound Recorder utility is used for creating and playing sound files and the Volume Control utility can be used to adjust sound levels.

- *System Administrative tools.* Windows NT provides a number of tools for maintaining the health of your computer over time. For example, the Backup accessory can be used to make backup copies of the files on your hard disk onto diskettes or magnetic tape. The Disk Administrator, Event Viewer, Performance Monitor, Remote Access Admin, User Manager, and Windows NT Diagnostics utilities are all available for helping you to manage and tweak your system's resources and performance. These tools are discussed in the Appendix.

When installing Windows NT, you choose the accessories you want to install onto the hard disk of your computer. Therefore, your computer may not contain the same accessories as your neighbor's computer. To see which accessory programs are installed on your computer, let's display the Accessories cascading menu.

Perform the following steps . . .

1. START: Programs, Accessories
   A list of accessory programs appears in the cascading menu, as shown in Figure 2.1. (*Note*: It is unlikely that your screen will appear identical to Figure 2.1. The menu options list the programs that are available on this computer. Your computer will have different menu options.)

FIGURE 2.1

THE PROGRAM, ACCESSORIES MENU

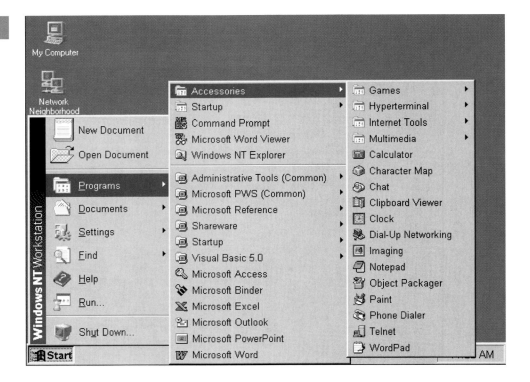

2. Point the mouse at the Administrative Tools (Common) menu option to see the utilities available for managing your system's resources.

3. To remove the menu and return to the desktop:
CLICK: *anywhere on the desktop's background*
(*Note*: If you don't have any desktop real estate that is available, you can also click the Start button (⊞Start) a second time to withdraw the menus.)

QUICK REFERENCE
Launching Program
Accessories and
System Utilities

- **To view the accessory programs available on your computer:**
  START: Programs, Accessories
- **To view the administrative tools available on your computer:**
  START: Programs, Administrative Tools (Common)

USING WORDPAD

Word processing is the most commonly used application for microcomputers. Using the WordPad word processing program, you can store, retrieve, edit, format, and print various types of documents. One significant advantage that word processing software programs have compared to typewriters is a feature called **word wrap.** Word wrap is the automatic process of moving the cursor to the next line when the end of the current line is reached. In other words, you type continuously without pressing the carriage return or **ENTER** key to advance to the next line. In Word-Pad, the **ENTER** key is used to end paragraphs and insert blank lines.

To load WordPad, you choose Programs, Accessories, WordPad from the Start menu. Once the program loads, you are presented with the WordPad window (Figure 2.2), ready for typing information or retrieving a document file.

FIGURE 2.2

THE WORDPAD WINDOW

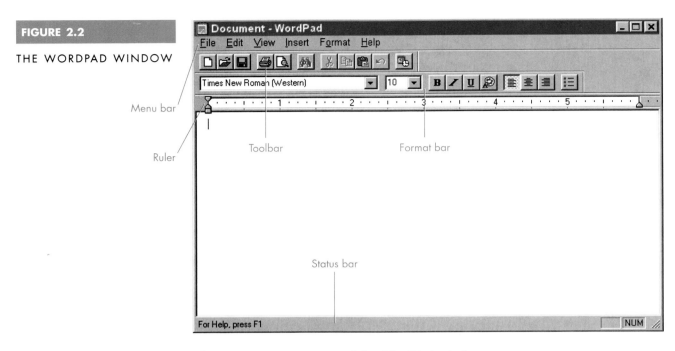

Menu bar

Ruler

Toolbar

Format bar

Status bar

The primary components of the WordPad window are:

Menu bar	Contains the WordPad menu commands.
Toolbar	The toolbar displays buttons for opening and saving documents, editing text, and accessing special features using the mouse. We label the toolbar buttons below:

Format bar	The Format bar displays buttons for accessing special character and paragraph formatting commands using the mouse. We label the Format bar below:

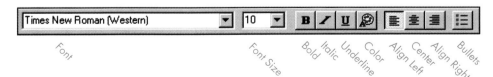

Ruler	The Ruler provides information about tab settings, paragraph indentations, and margins.
Status bar	Located on the bottom of the WordPad window, the Status bar displays command descriptions and indicates whether you've pressed a special key such as the **CAPS** key.

If you don't see the toolbar, Format bar, Ruler, and Status bar on your screen, choose View from the Menu bar and make sure a check mark (✔) appears next to these items in the pull-down menu.

CREATING A DOCUMENT

Creating a document in WordPad is easy. You type information onto the screen, save the document to the disk, and then send it to the printer. Before entering text into the document, make sure that you have a blinking cursor (also called an **insertion point**) in the upper left-hand corner of the WordPad window. This marks the location where text is inserted.

In the next few sections, you create the document pictured in Figure 2.3.

FIGURE 2.3

"PRACTICE PARAGRAPH - SESSION 2" DOCUMENT

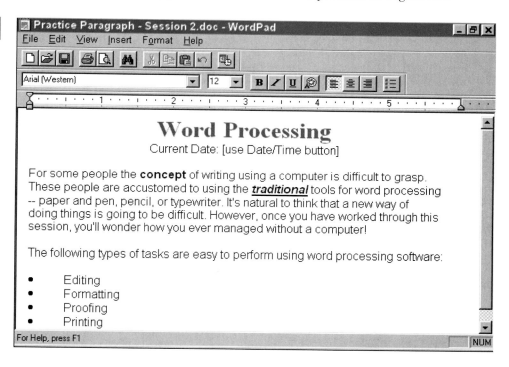

You start creating a document by entering the text. Later in this session, you will format the text and prepare it for printing.

Perform the following steps . . .

1. START: Programs, Accessories, WordPad

2. To maximize the window:
   CLICK: Maximize button (▢)

3. TYPE: Word Processing

4. To insert a blank line below the heading:
   PRESS: (ENTER) once

5. TYPE: Current Date:
PRESS: Space bar
In the next step, you will use the Date/Time button on the toolbar to insert the current date.

6. CLICK: Date/Time button (🖳)
SELECT: *any date format from the list that appears*
CLICK: OK or PRESS: **ENTER**

7. To insert a blank line between the heading and the body text:
PRESS: **ENTER** twice

8. TYPE: For some people the concept of writing using a computer is difficult to grasp. These people are accustomed to using the traditional tools for word processing -- paper and pen, pencil, or typewriter. It's natural to think that a new way of doing things is going to be difficult. However, once you have worked through this session, you'll wonder how you ever managed without a computer!
(*Note*: If you make a mistake when you are typing the text, press **BACKSPACE** to erase the mistake and then retype the correct text. To correct previous mistakes, position the insertion point to the left of the word that you want to remove and press **DELETE** several times until the word disappears. When you type in the new word, the existing text is pushed to the right.)

9. To continue adding another paragraph:
PRESS: **ENTER** twice
TYPE: The following types of tasks are easy to perform using word processing software:
PRESS: **ENTER** twice
TYPE: Editing
PRESS: **ENTER**
TYPE: Formatting
PRESS: **ENTER**
TYPE: Proofing
PRESS: **ENTER**
TYPE: Printing

10. PRESS: **ENTER**

QUICK REFERENCE	
QUICK REFERENCE Creating a Document Using WordPad	**1.** **START: Programs, Accessories, WordPad** **2.** **TYPE: *the desired text into the blank document that appears*** **3.** **PRESS: ENTER to start a new paragraph** **4.** **PRESS: BACKSPACE to correct typing errors as they occur**

SAVING A DOCUMENT

When you create or edit a document, you are working in the computer's temporary memory. To permanently store your work in a file on a disk, you click the Save button on the toolbar or choose File, Save from the Menu bar. You are then prompted by WordPad to name your file. When naming a file, you can use up to 255 characters, including spaces. However, you can't use the following special characters in filenames:

In the next few steps, you will save the practice paragraph to one of the following locations:

- *Advantage Files location*   This location may be on a diskette, a folder on your local hard drive, or a folder on a network server. The Advantage Files are the workbook files that have been created for you and that you will retrieve in the remaining exercises in this guide.

- *Data Files location*   This location may also be on a diskette, a hard drive folder, or a network folder. You will save the workbooks that you create or modify in the Data Files location.

> **IMPORTANT:** *Before continuing, ensure that you know the location of your Advantage Files and where to store your Data Files. If necessary, ask your instructor or lab assistant for additional information.*

Let's save the current document to your Data Files location.

Perform the following steps . . .

1. Make sure that you have identified the location for storing your data files. If you require a diskette, place it into the diskette drive now.

2. Position the mouse pointer over the Save button (📇) but do not click the left mouse button yet. When the pointer is stationary for a second, a ToolTip label appears with the button's name. ToolTips are handy for previewing the buttons on the Toolbar and Format bar.

3. CLICK: Save button (📇)
   The Save As dialog box (Figure 2.4) appears.

FIGURE 2.4

THE SAVE AS
DIALOG BOX

4. To choose where you want to save the file:
CLICK: down arrow beside the *Save in* drop-down list box
SELECT: *your Data Files location*

5. To name the file:
DOUBLE-CLICK: "Document" in the *File name* text box to select it
TYPE: `Practice Paragraph – Session 2`

6. To ensure that the remaining exercises in this section work correctly, make sure "Word for Windows 6.0" appears in the *Save as type* list box.

7. To save the file, do the following in the Save As dialog box:
CLICK: Save command button or PRESS: `ENTER`
You will hear a noise from the diskette drive as your work is saved.

QUICK REFERENCE
Saving a WordPad
Document

1. **CLICK: Save button (🖫), or**
   CHOOSE: File, Save from the Menu bar
2. **CLICK: down arrow adjacent to the *Save in* drop-down list box**
3. **SELECT: *the disk on which to save the file***
4. **TYPE: *a name* into the *File name* text box**
5. **CLICK: Save command button**

IN ADDITION USING LONG FILENAMES IN DOS (AND WINDOWS 3.1)

Because DOS can't understand filenames that are longer than eight characters, it must change a Windows 95 or NT filename when accessed in MS-DOS mode. For example, the filename "Multitasking Document" would be changed to "MULTIT~1.DOC" in MS-DOS mode.

OPENING AN EXISTING DOCUMENT

To modify or print a document that is stored on a disk, you must first retrieve the file by clicking the Open button (⬚) on the toolbar or choosing File, Open from the Menu bar. Once the Open dialog box is displayed, you select the location of the file from the *Look in* drop-down list box. You then double-click the desired document name appearing in the file window.

Figure 2.5 shows the Open window after selecting the ⬚ 3½ Floppy drive (A:) option in the *Look in* drop-down list box. This graphic assumes that your Data Files location is also the Advantage Diskette.

FIGURE 2.5

THE OPEN DIALOG BOX

QUICK REFERENCE
Opening a Document

1. **CLICK: Open button (⬚), or**
   CHOOSE: File, Open from the Menu bar
2. **SELECT:** *a file location* **from the *Look in* drop-down list box**
3. **DOUBLE-CLICK:** *the desired document name*

IN ADDITION A QUICK WAY TO OPEN A DOCUMENT

From the Start menu, Windows provides an easy way to open a document that you worked with recently. You choose Start, Documents and then select the document you want

to open from the cascading menu that appears. By default, Windows NT displays the last 15 documents that you have opened in this menu.

SELECTING AND EDITING TEXT

Once text has been typed into a document, editing and formatting changes are made by first selecting the text and then issuing the appropriate command. Selected text always appears highlighted in reverse video. In other words, selected text would appear white on black if your video display is normally black on white. A selection may be comprised of letters, words, lines, paragraphs, or the entire document.

Moving Around a Document

There are better ways to move around a document than pressing the ⬆ and ⬇ cursor-movement keys. Although these keys work well in short documents, they are not efficient for multiple-page documents. For these documents, you should use the mouse and scroll bar. When a document is longer than a page, a scroll bar displays on the right side. To page down or up through a document, you click the mouse pointer on the scroll bar below or above the scroll box, respectively. You can also drag the scroll box along the scroll bar to move more than one page at a time. Clicking the arrowheads at the top and bottom of the scroll bar enables you to move the contents of the window one line at a time.

Selecting Text

WordPad provides a column in the left margin of the document window called the **Selection area.** Although invisible, this area provides shortcuts for selecting text using the mouse. When the mouse is moved into this area, the pointer changes from an I-beam to the right-pointing diagonal arrow (⤢). Some methods for selecting a word, line, paragraph, or the entire document using the mouse are summarized in Table 2.1. To extend the selection to include several words, lines, or paragraphs, make the initial selection and then hold down the left mouse button and drag the pointer over the desired text.

TABLE 2.1	Select	Description
Selecting Text Using a Mouse	Single letter	Drag the I-beam mouse pointer over the letter you want to select.
	Single word	Double-click the word using the I-beam mouse pointer.
	Block of text	Move the cursor to the beginning of the block of text. Hold down the **SHIFT** key and then click the I-beam pointer at the end of the block.
	Single line	Move the mouse pointer into the Selection area, beside the desired line. Click once using the arrow mouse pointer.
	Single paragraph	Move the mouse pointer into the Selection area, beside the desired paragraph. Double-click using the arrow mouse pointer.
	Entire document	Move the mouse pointer into the Selection area. Hold down the **CTRL** key and click once using the arrow mouse pointer.

You will now practice moving around and selecting text in the "Practice Paragraph - Session 2" document.

Perform the following steps . . .

1. To select a word, position the mouse pointer over the word "concept" in the first sentence and then do the following:

   DOUBLE-CLICK: left mouse button on the word "concept"
   The entire word will appear highlighted in reverse video.

2. To select the first line in the practice paragraph, position the mouse pointer in the Selection area next to the first line (starting with "For.") When the I-beam mouse pointer changes to a right-pointing arrow:
   CLICK: left mouse button once
   Notice that the entire line is highlighted and not just the first sentence.

3. To delete the selected block of text:
   PRESS: DELETE
   The highlighted block of text disappears and the remaining text flows into the paragraph to compensate for the missing line.

4. To reverse the last command:
   CLICK: Undo button ( ) on the toolbar
   The text reappears in the first line. (*Note:* You can also use the Edit, Undo command on the Menu bar.)

5. To practice using the keyboard for moving around a document:
   PRESS: HOME
   The insertion point moves to the beginning of the line.

6. To move the insertion point to the end of a line:
   PRESS: END

7. To move to the bottom end of the document:
   PRESS: CTRL + END

8. To move to the beginning of the document:
   PRESS: CTRL + HOME

QUICK REFERENCE
Deleting Text

1. **SELECT:** *desired text that you want removed*
2. **PRESS:** DELETE, or
   CHOOSE: Edit, Clear

QUICK REFERENCE
Using the Undo Command

To cancel the last command performed, do the following:
- **CLICK: Undo button ( ), or**
- **CHOOSE: Edit, Undo**

FORMATTING TEXT

In WordPad, formatting a document refers to applying character and paragraph formatting options to text. This section describes and illustrates these two types of formatting.

Character Formatting

Enhancing text is referred to as character formatting. Specifically, character formatting involves selecting typefaces, font sizes, and styles for text. Some of the styles available in WordPad include bold, italic, underline, and strikeout. WordPad's character formatting commands are accessed through the Format, Font command (Figure 2.6), the Format bar, and shortcut menus. You display a shortcut menu by pointing to or selecting text in the document area and then clicking the right mouse button.

FONT DIALOG BOX

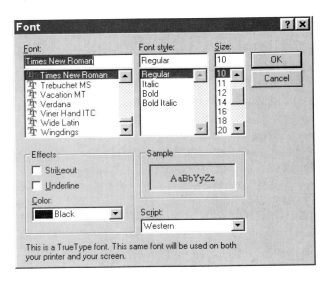

Paragraph Formatting

Paragraph formatting involves changing indentation, alignment, and tab settings for a paragraph. In WordPad, you can also add bullets to items in a list. WordPad's paragraph formatting commands are accessed through the Menu bar (Format, Paragraph and Format, Tab), the Format bar, and shortcut menus.

Let's format the practice document.

Perform the following steps . . .

1. Ensure that "Practice Paragraph - Session 2" appears in the WordPad window.

2. To practice enhancing text, select the word "difficult" in the first sentence and then do the following:
   CLICK: Bold button (**B**) on the Format bar
   The selection is bold and the text remains highlighted.

3. To italicize the same word:
   CLICK: Italic button (*I*) on the Format bar
   The selection is now italicized and bold.

4. To underline the word "traditional" in the second sentence, select the text and then do the following:
   CLICK: Underline button (U)

5. To make the heading "Word Processing" bold and underlined, select the text and then do the following:
CLICK: Bold button (**B**)
CLICK: Underline button (**U**)

6. To center both lines of the heading, select both lines and then do the following:
CLICK: Center button (≣)

7. To practice adding bullets, select the four word processing features located at the end of the document and then do the following:
CLICK: Bullets button (≣)
CLICK: anywhere in your document to remove the highlighting

8. To change the typeface and font size for the entire document, you must first select all of the text:
CHOOSE: Edit, Select All
Your document should appear highlighted.

9. CHOOSE: Format, Font
SELECT: Arial from the *Font* list box
SELECT: Regular from the *Font style* list box
SELECT: 12 from the *Size* list box
CLICK: OK command button

10. To remove the highlighting:
CLICK: *anywhere in the document*
Notice that the Bold and Italic styles are reset to Regular. Because the underlining is not considered a font style, the formatting remains intact.

11. To make the title "Word Processing" stand out a little more, select the text and then do the following:
CHOOSE: Format, Font
CLICK: *Underline* check box to remove the "✔"
SELECT: Times New Roman from the *Font* list box
SELECT: Bold from the *Font style* list box
SELECT: 24 from the *Size* list box

12. To change the color of text:
CLICK: down arrow to the right of the *Color* drop-down list box
SELECT: Maroon as the color
CLICK: OK command button
The formatting is applied to the title, but it remains highlighted.

13. To remove the highlighting:
CLICK: *anywhere in the document*

14. As a final step:
SELECT: "concept" in the first sentence
CLICK: Bold button (B)
SELECT: "traditional" in the second sentence
CLICK: Bold button (B)
CLICK: Italic button (I)
CLICK: *anywhere in the document*
Your document should now appear similar to Figure 2.2.

15. Save the document and overwrite the existing version using the Save button (🖫).

QUICK REFERENCE	
Character Formatting	**1. SELECT:** *desired text for formatting*
	2. CLICK: *a toolbar button* on the Format bar, or
	CHOOSE: Format, Font to display the Font dialog box

QUICK REFERENCE	
Paragraph Formatting	**1. Position the cursor in the paragraph to be formatted.**
	2. CLICK: *a toolbar button* on the Format bar, or
	CHOOSE: Format, Paragraph to display the Paragraph dialog box

PAGE SETUP

Before printing a document, you may want to change the document's margins or print orientation. You can accomplish these tasks using the Page Setup dialog box (Figure 2.7). WordPad provides the default settings of 1.25 inches for the left and right margins and 1 inch for the top and bottom margins. With respect to paper size, you can choose letter- or legal-sized paper with a **portrait orientation** (8.5 inches wide by 11 inches or 14 inches tall) or a **landscape orientation** (11 inches or 14 inches wide by 8.5 inches tall). You should note that WordPad remembers these Page Setup settings and automatically applies them to the next document you create. To display the Page Setup dialog box, you choose File, Page Setup from the Menu bar.

FIGURE 2.7

PAGE SETUP
DIALOG BOX

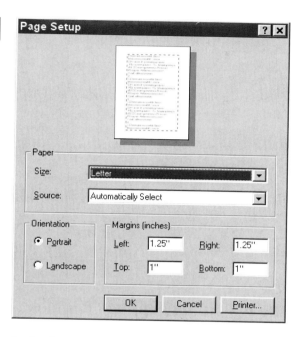

Let's change the left and right margins of the "Practice Paragraph - Session 2" document.

Perform the following steps . . .

1. CHOOSE: File, Page Setup from the Menu bar

2. To set the left and right margins to 1.75 inches:
   SELECT: the number in the *Left* margin text box by double-clicking it
   TYPE: 1.75
   SELECT: the number in the *Right* margin box by double-clicking it
   TYPE: 1.75
   Notice that the preview area near the top of the dialog box updates automatically to reflect the changes.

3. CLICK: OK or PRESS: (ENTER)
   Note that the symbols on the Ruler have moved to show the new margin settings.

4. On your own, change the margin settings to 1.25 inches for the top, bottom, left, and right margins.

QUICK REFERENCE
Using Page Setup

1. **CHOOSE: File, Page Setup from the Menu bar**
2. **Define new margins, a paper size, and/or a print orientation.**
3. **CLICK: OK or PRESS: (ENTER) to continue**

PRINTING A DOCUMENT

Now that you've learned how to create and format a document, this section explains how to send your document to the printer.

The quickest method for printing a document is to click the Print button (🖨) on the toolbar. When you click this button, no dialog boxes appear asking you to confirm your choice, so ensure that the printer is online and has sufficient paper. However, you may want to save a few trees by previewing the document on screen first using the Print Preview button (🔍). You can always click the Print button from the Print Preview screen if you want to send the document to the printer, after all.

Assuming that you have a printer connected to your computer or to the network, let's see what the document will look like when printed.

Perform the following steps . . .

1. To display a preview of the "Practice Paragraph - Session 2" document:
   CLICK: Print Preview button (🔍)

2. Carefully survey the document in Print Preview mode by clicking the magnifying glass mouse pointer in the page area. If you keep clicking the mouse, the view is automatically zoomed and shrunk in a cycle.

3. To leave the Print Preview mode:
   CLICK: Close button (❎)
   (*Note*: You can also click the Print button from this screen. For this exercise, we close the Print Preview mode in order to demonstrate the Print button on the toolbar.)

4. Assuming that you are pleased with the Print Preview results:
   CLICK: Print button (🖨)
   The "Practice Paragraph - Session 2" document will print to your default printer.

QUICK REFERENCE
Quick Printing

- **CLICK: Print Preview button (🔍) to see a preview of your document and then click the Print command button, or**
- **CLICK: Print button (🖨) to send your document directly to the printer**

LEAVING WORDPAD

When you are finished using WordPad, save your work and exit the program.

Perform the following steps . . .

1. To exit WordPad:
   CHOOSE: File, Exit

2. If you have made modifications to the current document, a dialog box appears asking for confirmation. Save your work and then exit the program.

USING PAINT

The Paint accessory enables you to create, modify, and save graphic pictures, including drawings, scanned images, and screen captures. You can print these graphics directly from Paint or you can paste them into documents created using other applications, such as WordPad, Microsoft Word, or Adobe PageMaker. To load Paint and display a blank canvas, you choose Programs, Accessories, and then Paint from the Start menu.

The Paint window (Figure 2.8) consists of the following components: Tool Box, Color Box, Pattern Area, Status bar, and Canvas. The Tool Box contains icons for drawing and filling shapes, typing text, and erasing elements. Depending on which tool you've chosen in the Tool Box, a selection of styles will appear in the Pattern Area below. In a color picture, Paint provides a color palette. In a monochrome picture, Paint provides a pattern palette. You choose a foreground color/pattern by pointing at the desired option and clicking the left mouse button. You select a background color/pattern by pointing at the desired option and clicking the right mouse button. When you first load Paint, the Pencil tool is chosen by default. To change the selected tool, you click on the desired icon in the Tool Box. To display the name of a tool, you simply rest the mouse pointer on a button until a ToolTip appears.

FIGURE 2.8

PAINT WINDOW

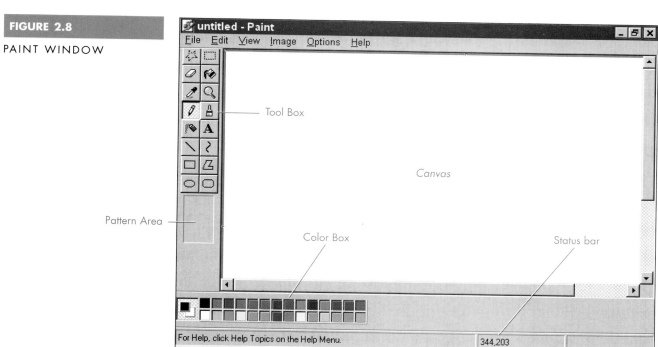

In this exercise, you create a simple graphic that illustrates the development cycle for software production. Your graphic will look like the one displayed in Figure 2.9.

DRAWING AN
ILLUSTRATION
USING PAINT

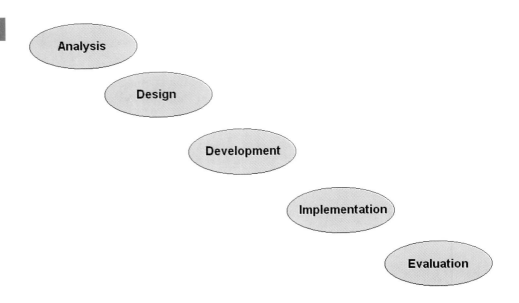

Perform the following steps . . .

1. START: Programs, Accessories, Paint

2. Maximize the Paint application window, if it isn't already.

3. CLICK: Ellipse tool ( )

4. Near the top left corner of the canvas:
   DRAG: the cross-hair mouse pointer down and to the right in order to create the first "bubble"

5. To apply a color to the interior of the bubble:
   CLICK: cyan square in the middle of the Color box
   CLICK: Fill With Color tool ( )
   (*Note*: Make sure that you click the color using the left mouse button.)

6. Position the paint can mouse pointer inside the ellipse and then click the left mouse button once to fill the interior with the new color.

7. To select this object:
   CLICK: Select tool ( )

8. Start in the upper left-hand corner and then drag a rectangle surrounding the ellipse. Selection handles and a frame will appear around the ellipse, if done correctly.

9. To move the selected object, position the mouse pointer over a part of the frame until a black cross with four arrows appears. Do not place it over a selection handle or box on the frame.

10. DRAG: the object until it is positioned exactly where you want it

11. With the object still selected:
    CHOOSE: Edit, Copy
    CHOOSE: Edit, Paste
    A new copy of the object appears in the upper left-hand corner.

12. Using the black cross mouse pointer, move the new object beside and below the first object by dragging its frame.

13. On your own, create and then position three more copies of the ellipse to appear similar to Figure 2.9.

14. Let's add a text caption to the first bubble object:
CLICK: Text tool (**A**)
CLICK: black square in the Color box using the left mouse button
DRAG: a rectangle that appears inside the first ellipse
An insertion point will appear in the framed area and the Text or Fonts toolbar will display, as shown here. (*Note*: If the Fonts toolbar does not display, choose the View, Text Toolbar command from the menu.)

15. In the Fonts dialog box:
SELECT: Arial for the Font
SELECT: 12 for the Font size
CLICK: Bold button (**B**)

16. TYPE: Analysis

17. To finalize the placement of text, position the white arrow mouse pointer over the text border frame and then drag the text into position.

18. On your own, add the remaining text captions to the bubbles as shown in Figure 2.9.

19. When you are satisfied with your creation, save the graphic:
CHOOSE: File, Save As from the Menu bar
CLICK: down arrow adjacent to the *Save in* drop-down list box
SELECT: *your Data Files location*

20. To specify the format and name of the file:
DOUBLE-CLICK: "untitled" in the *File name* text box to select it
TYPE: Cycle
CLICK: down arrow adjacent to the *Save as type* drop-down list box
SELECT: 16 Color Bitmap
CLICK: Save command button

21. To print your creation:
CHOOSE: File, Print Preview

22. If you are pleased with the drawing:
CLICK: Print command button under the Title bar
CLICK: OK command button

For more practice, create a map like the one displayed in Figure 2.10. (*Note*: Feel free to create a map of a different country.)

FIGURE 2.10

DRAWING A MAP
USING PAINT

MAP

IN ADDITION SHARING DATA BETWEEN APPLICATIONS

Using Paint, you can create a corporate logo for printing or a banner for your home page on the Internet. Whatever your demands, accessory programs like Paint can

serve objects and data to other higher-end applications. For example, the logo or banner that you create in Paint can be copied to the Clipboard and then pasted into an Adobe PageMaker or Microsoft Publisher document for final production.

USING OTHER ACCESSORIES

This section highlights several Windows NT accessories that you can explore on your own time. To load these programs, you choose Programs, Accessories from the Start menu and then select the accessory you want to use. Although not an exhaustive discussion of the accessory programs, this section highlights some of the most commonly used applications. You may want to load each application as it is discussed, but make sure that you close it before proceeding to the next accessory. (*Note*: All of the following accessories might not be installed on your computer.)

 Calculator

The Calculator accessory provides both a general and scientific version of a standard desktop calculator. You use Calculator to perform quick calculations while working in other application programs. For example, you could use Calculator to multiply an invoice amount by a tax rate when creating an invoice in WordPad. The results of any calculation can be copied to the Windows NT Clipboard for pasting into other documents or applications. See Figure 2.11.

FIGURE 2.11

CALCULATOR IN
SCIENTIFIC VIEW

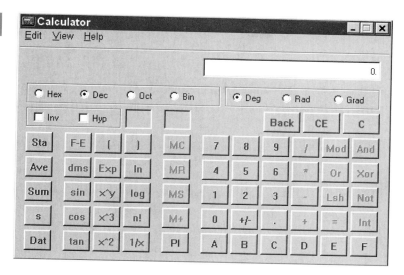

Clipboard Viewer

This utility lets you view information that you've copied or cut to the Windows **Clipboard**. Because Clipboard is only a temporary storage location in the computer's random access memory (RAM), you lose its contents each time you turn off the computer. Also, Clipboard only holds one piece of data at a time. When you copy new data to Clipboard, the existing data is cleared. To store the contents of Clipboard permanently, you must save it to your computer's "Local ClipBook." Using a ClipBook, you can create and store several pieces of data, each on its own page, and then share the entire ClipBook as a resource with other users on your network.

Dial-Up Networking

Over 50 percent of office workers use a computer that is part of a network, enabling them to exchange e-mail, access shared files, and share printers. For many people, the major disadvantage of working at home is that they don't have access to their office network. With Dial-Up Networking, you can connect to your office's network from your home computer. You can also use Dial-Up Networking with the TCP/IP Internet protocol to log on to your Internet Service Provider. This utility is often referred to as the client version of the Windows NT Remote Access Service (RAS).

HyperTerminal

The HyperTerminal accessory[1] enables you to communicate with another computer or communication service, such as AT&T Mail, MCI Mail, or CompuServe. You can use this accessory to connect to a computer Bulletin Board Service (BBS) or to transfer files between two remote computers. To launch HyperTerminal, choose Start, Programs, Accessories, HyperTerminal and then select the location to dial from the cascading menu.

Notepad

As a text editor, the Windows Notepad program does not provide sophisticated word processing capabilities like those available in WordPad. With Notepad, you create, save, and print Batch Files (BAT), System Files (SYS), web page documents

---

[1]The Windows NT HyperTerminal accessory replaces the Windows 3.1 Terminal accessory.

using the HyperText Markup Language (HTML), and other **ASCII** text files (unformatted files containing characters from the American Standard Code for Information Interchange). It is designed primarily to create simple text files consisting of line item entries. For larger text files, you should use the WordPad accessory for viewing or to make modifications and then save the file as a Text document, instead of the default Word 6.0 format. See Figure 2.12.

FIGURE 2.12

USING NOTEPAD TO
DISPLAY A WEB PAGE
DOCUMENT

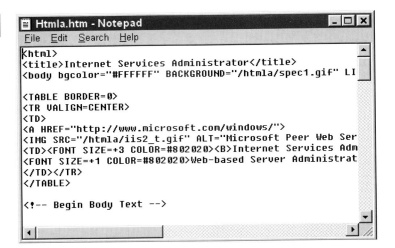

```
Htmla.htm - Notepad
File   Edit   Search   Help
<html>
<title>Internet Services Administrator</title>
<body bgcolor="#FFFFFF" BACKGROUND="/htmla/spec1.gif" LI

<TABLE BORDER=0>
<TR VALIGN=CENTER>
<TD>
<A HREF="http://www.microsoft.com/windows/">
<IMG SRC="/htmla/iis2_t.gif" ALT="Microsoft Peer Web Ser
<TD><FONT SIZE=+3 COLOR=#802020><B>Internet Services Adm
<FONT SIZE=+1 COLOR=#802020>Web-based Server Administrat
</TD></TR>
</TABLE>

<!-- Begin Body Text -->
```

Phone Dialer

This accessory enables you to dial the phone and make voice calls from your computer. Phone Dialer also enables you to program numbers for speed dialing. To use Phone Dialer, you need a phone line connected to the Line In socket of your computer's modem and a telephone connected to the Line Out socket. After you place a call from your computer, Phone Dialer directs you to pick up your telephone's receiver in order to transfer the call from the modem to your telephone.

Telnet

This accessory lets you connect to a port or service on the Internet. Before launching this accessory program, you use the Dial-Up Networking program to establish a connection with your Internet Service Provider. Once you are connected to the remote system, you can telnet or travel the Internet and access many sites from around the world. (*Note*: You typically need an account or logon name and password to gain full access to telnet sites on the Internet.)

In addition to these accessory programs, there are several administrative tools in Windows NT for managing your disk storage areas and network connections. To access these tools, you choose the Start, Administrative Tools (Common) command. The cascading menu that appears may include the following choices:

- Backup
- Disk Administrator
- Event Viewer
- Performance Monitor
- Remote Access Admin
- User Manager
- Windows NT Diagnostics

Several of these important tools are detailed in the Appendix.

Multitasking

With NT Workstation's multitasking capabilities, you can execute multiple applications concurrently without a noticeable degradation in performance. Besides saving time, multitasking facilitates the exchange of data among applications. As mentioned in the previous section, information that you cut or copy from an application is placed in a special area of memory called the Clipboard. You can paste the contents of the Clipboard to another location in the same application or to another running application.

In the following exercise, you create the document shown in Figure 2.13 using the WordPad, Calculator, and Paint accessories.

FIGURE 2.13

MULTITASKING
DOCUMENT

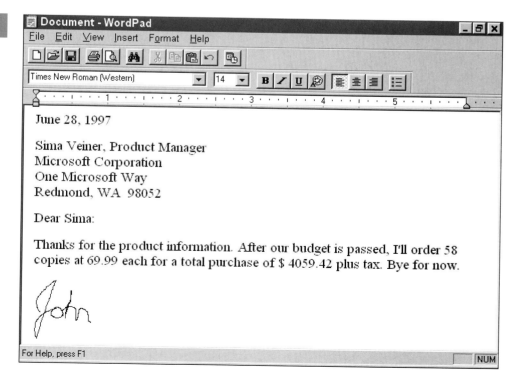

Document - WordPad

File   Edit   View   Insert   Format   Help

Times New Roman (Western)   14   B / U

June 28, 1997

Sima Veiner, Product Manager
Microsoft Corporation
One Microsoft Way
Redmond, WA 98052

Dear Sima:

Thanks for the product information. After our budget is passed, I'll order 58 copies at 69.99 each for a total purchase of $ 4059.42 plus tax. Bye for now.

For Help, press F1   NUM

Perform the following steps . . .

1. Ensure that there are no open windows on the desktop.

2. To load the Calculator, Paint, and WordPad accessories:
   START: Programs, Accessories, Calculator
   START: Programs, Accessories, Paint
   START: Programs, Accessories, WordPad

3. To organize the three windows on the desktop:
   RIGHT-CLICK: *an empty area on the taskbar*
   CHOOSE: Cascade

4. To switch to WordPad and maximize its window:
   CLICK: WordPad button on the taskbar
   CLICK: its Maximize button (□)

5. Using a Times New Roman font of 14 points in size, type the text appearing in the document area of Figure 2.13 up to and including the dollar sign ($). You will calculate the bill total (4059.42) in the next step using the Calculator and then complete the document.

6. To switch to Calculator:
   CLICK: Calculator button on the taskbar
   CLICK: 58 on the number pad
   CLICK: *
   CLICK: 69.99 on the number pad
   CLICK: =
   The answer should appear in its display window.

7. To copy the answer into the WordPad document:
   CHOOSE: Edit, Copy from the Calculator Menu bar
   CLICK: WordPad button on the taskbar

8. Make sure that the insertion point or cursor is positioned immediately to the right of the dollar sign ($). Then, do the following:
   CLICK: Paste button (▣) on the toolbar
   PRESS: Space bar

9. Finish typing the remainder of the letter as displayed in Figure 2.13. When finished, do the following:
   PRESS: (ENTER) twice
   Next, you'll copy a signature from the Paint accessory program.

10. CLICK: Paint button on the taskbar

11. Using the Pencil tool, sign your name on the canvas by dragging the mouse pointer like a pencil.

12. CLICK: Select tool (▣) from the Tool Box

13. Position the mouse pointer at the top-left corner of your signature:
CLICK: left mouse button and hold it down
DRAG: mouse pointer to the bottom right-hand corner so that the rectangle surrounds the entire signature
(*Note:* Do not include too much white space in the selection.)

14. Release the mouse button.

15. To copy the outlined graphic to the Clipboard:
CHOOSE: Edit, Copy from the Paint Menu bar

16. CLICK: WordPad button on the taskbar

17. To paste the signature into the WordPad document:
CLICK: Paste button (📇) on the toolbar
CLICK: *another part of the document to remove the selection box*
The document should now look similar to Figure 2.13.

18. To save the WordPad document:
CLICK: Save button (💾) on the toolbar

19. To choose where you want to save the file:
CLICK: down arrow adjacent to the *Save in* drop-down list box
SELECT: *your Data Files location*

20. To name the file:
DOUBLE-CLICK: "document" in the *File name* text box to select it
TYPE: `Multitasking Document`
CLICK: Save command button

Leave all of the applications open for our discussion of the Task Manager in the next section.

QUICK REFERENCE Moving and Copying Information Using the Clipboard	• **To move information into the Clipboard:** **CLICK: Cut button (✂) or CHOOSE: Edit, Cut** • **To copy information into the Clipboard:** **CLICK: Copy button (📇) or CHOOSE: Edit, Copy** • **To paste information from the Clipboard:** **CLICK: Paste button (📇) or CHOOSE: Edit, Paste**

TASK MANAGER

The Windows NT Task Manager lets you monitor the programs and system **processes** that are running on your computer. Each program or process that runs in the NT multitasking environment may also have several **threads** running at the same time. For example, you can send a Print command (one thread) to Microsoft Word 97 and then continue spell checking the document (another thread). Because more than one thread is active in this application, it is referred to as a *multi-threaded* application. In addition to letting you manage the running programs and processes, the Task Manager analyzes and displays a real-time graphical report card for your system.

In this exercise, you practice using the Task Manager.

Perform the following steps . . .

1. Ensure that the Calculator, Paint, and WordPad applications are still running on the desktop.

2. Before launching the Task Manager, let's practice moving among the open applications using a shortcut method. Make sure that the WordPad application window is maximized and active. Then, do the following to peruse the other open applications:
PRESS: **ALT** and hold it down
PRESS: **TAB** once
You must keep the **ALT** key depressed. Otherwise, you will move to the application whose icon is highlighted in the message board.

3. To move to Calculator with the **ALT** key still depressed:
PRESS: **TAB** key to highlight the Calculator icon
RELEASE: **ALT** key
The Calculator window should now appear on top of the WordPad application window.

4. Using **ALT**+**TAB**, change the active application to Paint.

5. Using **ALT**+**TAB**, change the active application to WordPad.

6. Let's launch the Task Manager:
RIGHT-CLICK: *an empty area on the taskbar*
CHOOSE: Task Manager
The Task Manager window appears on top of the WordPad window. The first tab, called *Applications*, is selected and displays a list of the applications that are currently running.

7. To see a performance analysis of your system:
CLICK: *Performance* tab
This tab displays the CPU and Memory Usage of your computer with history graphs. Also, there are summaries provided for Physical, Virtual, and Kernel Memory statistics. Your screen should now look similar, but not identical, to Figure 2.14.

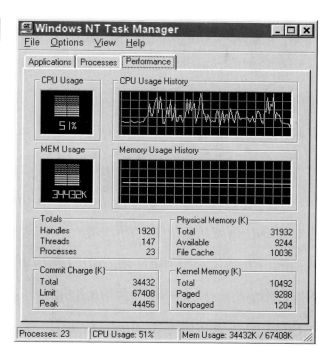

FIGURE 2.14

TASK MANAGER:
PERFORMANCE TAB

8. To see which programs and processes are loaded into memory:
CLICK: *Processes* tab

9. Let's make sure that you are viewing all the necessary columns:
CHOOSE: View, Select Columns

10. Ensure that the following options are selected:
SELECT: *PID (Process Identifier)* check box
SELECT: *CPU Usage* check box
SELECT: *CPU Time* check box
SELECT: *Memory Usage* check box
CLICK: OK command button to remove the dialog box

11. In the list box:
CLICK: *Image Name* column header to sort the list
SELECT: mspaint.exe
Notice the amount of memory being used by the Paint accessory program. This tab provides some important information for explaining why certain programs run slowly. For example, they may consume more resources than other programs.

12. Let's close an application using the Task Manager:
CLICK: *Applications* tab
SELECT: Calculator
Notice that Calculator's status column shows that it is running.

13. To close the Calculator program:
CLICK: End Task command button
The Calculator entry is immediately removed from the list. (*Note*: This exercise demonstrates how to use the Task Manager for closing an errant or frozen application that is not responding to a normal File, Exit command. You should not make a general practice of closing applications using the Task Manager.)

14. To close the Task Manager:
CLICK: its Close button (🗙)

15. Close all of the open windows on the desktop. If asked to save your changes, click the No command button.

16. Shut down your computer or log off, if you are finished for the session.

QUICK REFERENCE	
Using the Task Manager	**1.** RIGHT-CLICK: *an empty area on the taskbar*
	2. CLICK: *Applications* tab to display a list of the running programs and to close errant or frozen applications
	3. CLICK: *Processes* tab to display statistics for each running process, including the memory used by a particular application
	4. CLICK: *Performance* tab to display CPU and memory usage statistics

SUMMARY

This session introduced you to some of the accessories that accompany Windows NT Workstation. You learned how to use WordPad—a word processing program, and Paint—a drawing program. Besides writing and drawing accessories, Windows NT includes communications and multimedia programs and a number of administrative system tools for maintaining your computer. You also learned how to use the Clipboard to share data among Windows NT applications. The session concluded with a lesson on using the Task Manager to manage your running programs and to analyze the performance of your computer system.

COMMAND SUMMARY

Many of the commands and procedures appearing in this session are provided in the command summary in Table 2.2.

	Task Description	General Instruction
TABLE 2.2 Command Summary	Saving a WordPad Document	Click the Save button () and then select a disk drive and filename.
	Opening a File in drive WordPad	Click the Open button () and then select a disk and filename.
	Character Formatting in WordPad	Select the text and then click the Bold (**B**), Italic (*I*), or Underline (U) buttons on the Format bar.
	Paragraph Formatting WordPad	Select the text and then click an alignment button in () or the Bullets button () on the Format bar.
	Using Page Setup in WordPad	Choose File, Page Setup from the Menu bar.
	Previewing a Document in WordPad	Click the Print Preview button ().
	Printing a Document in WordPad	Click the Print button ().
	Sharing Information Between Applications	First, select the text or picture you want to copy or move. Click the Cut button () or Copy button () to move or copy the data. Position the cursor in the target document. Click the Paste button ().
	Displaying the Task Manager	Right-click an empty area of the taskbar and choose the Task Manager command from the pop-up menu.

KEY TERMS

ASCII

Acronym for American Standard Code for Information Interchange. An ASCII text file refers to an unformatted text file that is viewed or edited by DOS or using the Notepad accessory program.

Clipboard

In Windows, a program that allows you to copy and move information to a temporary storage location in memory and then paste the information into the same document or to another application.

insertion point

The vertical flashing bar in WordPad that indicates your current position in the document (also referred to as a cursor). The insertion point shows where the next typed characters will appear.

landscape orientation

Describes how a page is printed. Letter-size paper with a landscape orientation measures 11-inches wide by 8.5-inches high. Legal-size paper with a landscape orientation measures 14-inches wide by 8.5-inches high.

multimedia

This term refers to technology that presents information using different media at the same time, including text, graphics, animation, video, music, and voice.

portrait orientation

Describes how a page is printed. Letter-size paper with a portrait orientation measures 8.5 inches wide by 11 inches high. Legal-size paper with a portrait orientation measures 8.5 inches wide by 14 inches high.

processes

In Windows NT, programs that are running in memory; each process includes the executable program, the memory address space, and the program's *threads*.

Selection area

The leftmost column in the WordPad window; it provides shortcut methods for selecting text using the mouse.

threads

The part of an application or process that runs the program's instructions; for example, spell-checking a document or re-calculating a worksheet. Windows NT allows multithreaded applications to access more than one processor for enhanced multitasking performance.

word wrap

When the cursor reaches the right-hand margin of a line, it automatically wraps to the left margin of the next line; the user does not have to press a carriage return key at the end of each line to move the cursor down.

EXERCISES

SHORT ANSWER

1. Name the four categories of Windows NT accessory programs listed at the beginning of this session.

2. List some uses for the Selection area in a WordPad window.

3. What types of commands are described as character formatting commands? paragraph formatting commands?

4. In Paint, what are the file formats available for saving an illustration?

5. What two views are provided in the Calculator accessory program?

6. How does the Notepad accessory differ from WordPad?

7. What is the purpose of the Dial-Up Networking accessory?

8. What is the purpose of the Telnet accessory?

9. How would you store permanently information that exists only on the Clipboard?

10. How would you determine how much memory WordPad consumes when it is running?

HANDS-ON

(*Note*: Ensure that you know the storage location of your Advantage Files and your Data Files before proceeding.)

1. Using the WordPad accessory program, create the document appearing in Figure 2.15. Make sure to include your name in the closing of the letter. Save this document to your Data Files location as "Draft Letter to Juanita Pallos."

FIGURE 2.15

"DRAFT LETTER TO
JUANITA PALLOS"
DOCUMENT

March 14, 1997

Ms. Juanita Pallos
2910 S.W. Marine Drive
Suite 1201
Stanford, CA 94305

Dear Ms. Pallos:

Thank you for your letter regarding the upcoming
event. I am in complete agreement with you that the
number of persons attending must be limited to 350.
In addition, your idea of having this event catered
sounds fantastic!

Moving to a different subject, I noticed that the
letter you wrote me was typed using a typewriter.
With the number of letters you write, you really
should consider purchasing a microcomputer and word
processing software program.

If you are interested, I would be happy to show you
some word processing fundamentals. We could even
use my computer to design and print the invitations
for the event!

Best regards,

your name

a. Insert the following text (and bullets) between the second and third
   paragraphs:

   Specifically, word processing software makes it
   easier to change a document by allowing you to do
   the following:

   - Insert text
   - Delete text
   - Copy and move text
   - Format text

b. In the first line of the last paragraph, delete the words "If you are interested," and start the sentence with "If you can spare the time."

c. Save the document back to your Data Files location using the same filename.

d. Print the document.

e. Exit WordPad.

2. In this exercise, create the picture in Figure 2.16 using the Paint accessory. When you are finished, save the picture as "Accessories Pie Chart" to your Data Files location using a 16 Color Bitmap format. Send the picture to the printer, but do not exit Paint. The Paint accessory program is also used in the next exercise.

FIGURE 2.16

"ACCESSORIES PIE
CHART" DOCUMENT

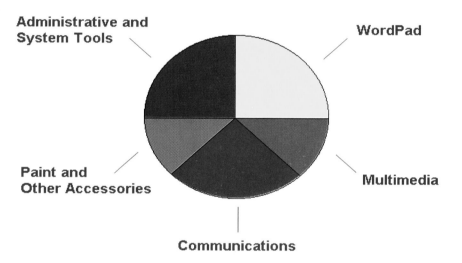

Windows NT Accessories

Administrative and System Tools

WordPad

Paint and Other Accessories

Multimedia

Communications

3. In this exercise, you practice sharing data between WordPad and Paint.

a. Create the document pictured in Figure 2.17 using WordPad.

b. Save the new document as "NT Accessory Programs" to your Data Files location.

c. Add two blank lines at the end of the paragraph.

d. Copy the pie chart named "Accessories Pie Chart" that you created in exercise 2 to the end of the memo.

e. Center the pie chart between the margins.

f. Save the completed document again under the same name.

FIGURE 2.17

"NT ACCESSORY
PROGRAMS" DOCUMENT

To: All Employees
        Allied Travel Corporation
Re: Windows NT Accessories

Some of you have submitted purchase requests for
software that is already stored on your computer.
Windows NT includes a number of accessories that
might fulfill your needs. Simply choose Programs,
Accessories from the Start menu to view a list of
the accessories that are stored on your computer.
We have categorized the different types of
accessories below. (*Note*: For more information,
read this session of the guide.)

4. **On Your Own:** Creating an Informal Report
   Using WordPad, describe your current hobby or favorite pursuit in a one- or
   two-page document. Create a formatted cover page that includes the title for
   your document, your name, and the current date. Review your document for
   spelling mistakes. After the review, use the print preview feature of Word-
   Pad to examine the document and then send it to the printer. Finally, you
   must save the document to your Data Files location as "My Life in Word-
   Pad" and exit WordPad.

5. **On Your Own:** Creating a Local Map
   Using Paint, create a map that shows people how to find your house or resi-
   dence in relation to the major centers in your area. Use the Color box to
   color-code the streets and landmarks on your map. Use the Text tool to provide instructions alongside the map. Save the illustration to your Data Files
   location as a 16 Color Bitmap named "To My House." Print the illustration
   and then exit Paint.

CASE PROBLEMS	ADVANCED SOFTWARE DESIGN, INC.

(*Note*: In the following case problems, assume the role of the primary characters and perform the same steps that they identify. You may want to reread the session opening.)

1. For the past year, Alethia's proposals have all looked similar to the one appearing in Figure 2.18. She wants to create a new document that contains the same information but with formatting enhancements. For example, she would like to make the company's name and address look more like a letterhead on printed stationery, perhaps centered and with a different font at the top of the page. She would also like to add emphasis to the different titles on the proposal (Date, Client Name, Project Description, and so on).

Using WordPad, create the document appearing in Figure 2.18 and then perform the steps that Alethia has identified. Print it and then save the document as "ASD Proposal" to your Data Files location. Once finished, close the WordPad accessory program.

FIGURE 2.18

A STANDARD ASD
PROPOSAL DOCUMENT

```
ADVANCED SOFTWARE DESIGN, INC.
221 FOREST DRIVE
Lakewood, NJ 08701
Tel: 630-555-4567
Fax: 630-555-5678

DATE: [enter current date]

CLIENT NAME: [enter client name]

PROJECT DESCRIPTION: [enter project description]

HOUR ESTIMATE: [enter hours]

COST ESTIMATE: [multiply the hours by $50]

Signature _____
              Alethia Montera
```

2. Alethia just finished a telephone conversation with Mountain Wear, Inc. She now wants to convert her scrawled notes into a proposal. The project description reads:

    Mountain Wear, Inc., a manufacturer of rugged footwear, needs a better program for keeping track of its inventory. It has one warehouse, with several truckloads of shoes coming and going each day. The company would like to generate hourly reports and gather demographic data on the people who buy Mountain Wear shoes. I estimate this job will take 122 programming hours.

    Alethia retrieves the "ASD Proposal" document from her Data Files location and edits it to include the information from her notes. To calculate the cost estimate, she minimizes the WordPad window and launches Calculator. After performing the calculation, she copies the result to the Clipboard and pastes it onto the appropriate line in the proposal. She prints and then saves the proposal to her Data Files location as "MWI Proposal," and then closes WordPad.

3. Upon returning to her office, Alethia finds a note tacked to her computer monitor from her boss, Iggy Simon. The note reads:

    Alethia, I need someone to create a splashy advertising piece for an upcoming customer mailing, and I think you're the one to do it now that you're so proficient in using Windows NT! I want you to make the following points: (1) Advanced Software Design can satisfy any programming requirement because of its staff of highly talented programmers, (2) ASD always supplies accurate cost estimates, (3) Your satisfaction is guaranteed—should you be dissatisfied with a product, we'll either modify it at our own cost or give you a full refund, (4) ASD provides a 24-hour support hotline should questions arise once an application is delivered.

    And lastly, I want you to create and paste a logo of a 3.5-inch diskette above our name and address at the top of the page. Also, Alethia, try to draw the reader's attention to the following line: The Small Business Association, in conjunction with the Hapstead Publishing Group, did an assessment of software development companies and gave Advanced Software Design the "Best Pick" award for 1996. By the way, I need this by tomorrow. Let me know if you have any questions. Thanks, Iggy.

    Although she's flattered, it's already late in the day and Alethia is concerned about completing the advertising piece on time. She realizes that without NT Workstation she wouldn't stand a chance at finishing this ad. When you do finish the project, print the document and then save it as "ASD Advertisement" to your Data Files location.

Microsoft Windows NT 4.0

Managing Files and Disks

SESSION

3

SESSION OUTLINE

INTRODUCTION

For the same reasons you arrange folders in a filing cabinet or organize your desk, you use folders to manage your work on disks. Using "My Computer" and the Windows NT Explorer, you can perform routine disk, folder, and file management tasks such as formatting diskettes, creating folders, copying files, or deleting an entire disk's contents.

BERKFORD COLLEGE, PENNSYLVANIA

Sharon Rheingold is a second-year law student at Berkford College in Pennsylvania. As a credit component toward her studies this semester, Sharon accepted a job teaching Public Speaking 101 to first-year business students. Given her goal of one day becoming a successful trial lawyer, Sharon saw this job as an opportunity to hone her communication skills on a captive audience. Little did she realize that Dr. Kirsten Antoski, the dean of Business Administration, had personally developed the course and expected each of her instructors to produce and submit outlines for each lecture. With an already suffocating course load, Sharon wonders how she can possibly create and manage course outlines for over 30 lectures this term.

While discussing the situation with Walt, her roommate, they stumble upon an especially good idea. Walt, a fourth-year student in the Faculty of Education, recommends that Sharon use the WordPad accessory to jot down course outline ideas and store them on her computer. With only a few tips on file and folder management, Walt assures her, keeping track of 30 or more files using "My Computer" or the Windows NT Explorer will be easy.

In this session, you and Sharon learn the fundamentals of managing your computer files, folders, and disks using Windows NT. By the end of this session, you will be able to copy, delete, and rename files, create and remove directory folders, prepare new diskettes for storage, and share your files, folders, and disks on a network.

WHAT IS FILE MANAGEMENT?

File management is the process of managing the work that you create and store on hard disks and floppy diskettes. Each document that you create is stored in a disk file, similar to a file folder in a manual filing system. Managing your work involves copying, renaming, and deleting files.

There are three categories of files that appear on hard disks and floppy diskettes: program files, document files, and data files. **Program files** consist of computer instructions for performing a certain task or for running an application program. **Document files** and **data files** contain work that you create using an application program recognized by Windows. Document files whose type is not recognized by Windows are called data files. The file management principles discussed in this session apply equally to program, document, and data files.

WHAT IS DISK MANAGEMENT?

Disk management is the process of managing the storage areas in your computer. These storage areas can be vast. For example, one hard disk can store data that would normally fill several large filing cabinets. On a new disk, there is only one area for storing files: the **root directory.** From the root directory, you create additional storage areas called **folders.**

Think of the root directory as the top of the filing cabinet and each folder as a drawer or folder in the cabinet. If you continually place documents on top of the cabinet, the files will quickly reach the ceiling. One solution would be to move the files from the top of the filing cabinet into the cabinet drawers. On a computer, you move files from the root directory to folders on the hard disk. You can also create folders within folders. Disk management also involves preparing new disks for storing data, backing up data, ensuring the stability of disk drives, optimizing the performance of disk drives, and labeling or naming disks.

Windows provides two applications, or models, for managing your computer's disks, folders, and files. The two models differ more in presentation than in function. "My Computer" is the easier model to use for beginners, whereas NT Explorer is more efficient for intermediate to experienced users. We describe both of these applications in this session. Windows also includes an application called "Network Neighborhood," which enables you to manage the files on your network.

FILE- AND DISK-NAMING CONVENTIONS

A description of file-naming conventions for DOS or Windows 3.1 would be quite lengthy because of the strict rules you must follow. But now we can describe Windows NT's conventions in just two short sentences. When naming a file, you can use up to 255 characters, including spaces. The only characters that you are limited from using are: \ / : * ? " < > and | because Windows uses them for other purposes.

There are several possible disk drive configurations for microcomputers and knowing how to reference each storage device is very important, although less so than when using DOS and Windows 3.1. Windows NT uses icons and descriptive text in addition to a disk name to describe the storage devices in your computer system. The first diskette drive is always referred to as drive A:. If your computer has two diskette drives, drive A: is usually positioned to the left or above the second diskette drive in the computer case, called drive B:. If your computer has a hard disk drive, it is referred to as drive C: and located inside the computer case. Any subsequent drive in your computer system, such as another hard drive or a CD-ROM drive, is labeled with the next letter. For example, the next drive would be named drive D:. The drive letter is always followed by a colon (:) to represent a drive designation. If you are attached to a network, you may see drive mappings that proceed further up the alphabet.

USING "MY COMPUTER" TO MANAGE FILES

The "My Computer" application provides an easy model for managing the files on your computer. In the following sections, you use "My Computer" to copy and move files, rename files, and delete files. But first you need to know how to select folders and files and how to customize the "My Computer" window. This session assumes that you are using a 3.5-inch floppy diskette as your Advantage Files location. Your Data Files location may remain a different diskette, a local hard drive, or a network drive.

SELECTING FOLDERS AND FILES

"My Computer" is based on a "Select" and then "Do" approach whereby you highlight folders and files and then execute commands from the shortcut menu or Menu bar. When you double-click a folder, the sub-folders and files in that folder are displayed in an additional window. The name of each open window appears on the taskbar.

Table 3.1 summarizes the methods for selecting files.

TABLE 3.1

Selecting Files

To select this element . . .	*Perform this action . . .*
A single folder or file	Click the folder or file icon once using the left mouse button.
A group of files that are located next to each other	Using the mouse, you can drag the mouse pointer to place a rectangle around the group of files. When you release the mouse button, the files will be selected. Using a shortcut method, you can click the first item and then hold down the (SHIFT) key while selecting the last item.
A group of files that aren't located next to each other	Hold down the (CTRL) key and then click with the mouse on the items you want to select.

In this exercise, you practice selecting files using the mouse.

Perform the following steps . . .

1. Ensure that the Advantage Diskette is in drive A:. (*Note*: To successfully perform the exercises in this session, we assume that a 3.5-inch diskette provides your Advantage Files location.)

2. DOUBLE-CLICK: "My Computer" icon ( ) on the desktop
The "My Computer" window on your computer should look similar to Figure 3.1, although different icons will probably appear. Figure 3.1 shows that this computer contains a 3½ Floppy drive (A:), a hard disk named Comtex (C:), and a CD-ROM drive (D:). To distinguish each hard drive, you can give each drive in the computer a specific name. Also notice that Comtex (C:) is a *shared* drive, as shown by the hand placed under the drive icon in Figure 3.1. A shared drive allows other users on the network access to its resources. The CD-ROM drive is not shared in this graphic. You will learn how to share a computer's storage resources later in this session.

FIGURE 3.1

THE "MY COMPUTER"
WINDOW

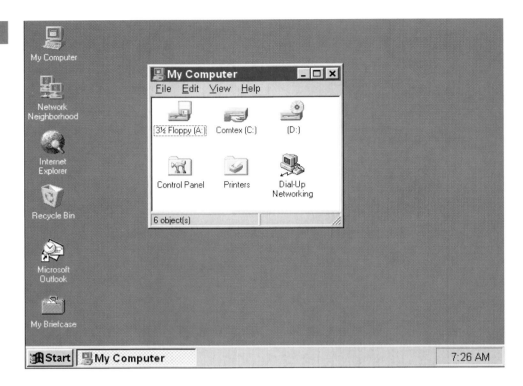

3. To view the files on the Advantage Diskette:
   DOUBLE-CLICK: 3½ Floppy drive (A:)
   A window showing the files in the root directory of drive A: should appear.
   The label "3½ Floppy (A:)" appears in the Title bar.

4. Maximize the drive A: window:
   CLICK: Maximize button ()

5. To modify the display of the window contents:
   RIGHT-CLICK: *an empty part of the window* (not on a file icon)
   CHOOSE: Arrange Icons, Auto Arrange
   With the Auto Arrange command enabled, the folder and file icons will line
   up automatically in the window, even after you size the window or copy,
   move, and delete icons. Windows remembers this Auto Arrange setting until
   you change it.

6. RIGHT-CLICK: *an empty part of the window* (not on a file icon)
   CHOOSE: View, Large Icons
   (*Note*: You learn more about changing the file view in the next section.) The
   window should now look similar, but not identical, to Figure 3.2. Depending
   on whether you saved the exercises in Session 2 to the Advantage Diskette,
   certain files may or may not be displayed as in Figure 3.2.

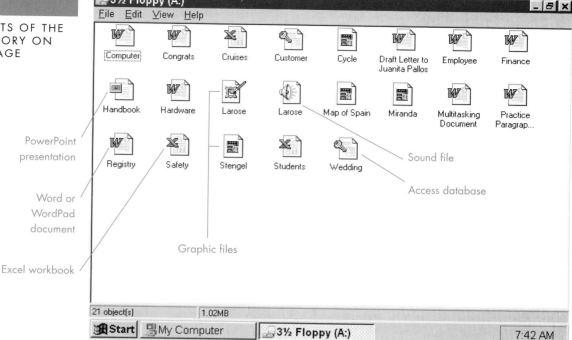

FIGURE 3.2

THE CONTENTS OF THE
ROOT DIRECTORY ON
THE ADVANTAGE
DISKETTE

7. To select a file, you point to the icon and click once. To edit a file, you point to the icon and double-click. By double-clicking an icon, you automatically load the source application, if available, and the file. In this exercise, let's just select the file named Cruises:
CLICK: Cruises file icon once
The file should be highlighted from the rest of the icons in the window. The icon appearing above the filename tells you which application was used to create the file. For example, all files created with Windows WordPad or Microsoft Word are displayed using the same icon (📝). Figure 3.2 points out some of the file icons and their source applications.

8. To deselect the file:
CLICK: *an empty part of the window*

9. To select the first four adjacent files in the second row, position the mouse pointer above and to the left of the first file and then hold down the left mouse button. Drag the mouse to the right and down until four files appear selected. (*Note:* As you may notice, you don't have to surround the files entirely with the rectangle in order to select them.)

10. Release the mouse button. The four files should appear highlighted.

11. To deselect the files:
CLICK: *an empty part of the window* using the left mouse button

12. To select two files that aren't next to each other:
CLICK: Stengel file icon
PRESS: (CTRL) and hold it down
CLICK: Hardware file icon
Both files should now appear highlighted.

13. Deselect the files by clicking an empty part of the window.

14. To select a series of contiguous files, click the first file in the top left-hand corner of the window. Then, do the following
PRESS: (SHIFT) and hold it down
CLICK: the last file on the first row in the top right-hand corner
All the files between the first click and the second click are selected.

15. Release the (SHIFT) key.

16. Deselect the files by clicking an empty part of the window. With the Advantage Diskette window still maximized on the screen, continue to the next section.

QUICK REFERENCE
Selecting Folders
and Files

- **CLICK:** *a file or folder icon* once to select a single file or folder
- **DRAG:** the mouse pointer across multiple icons to select a group of files or folders that appear next to each other in the window
- Use (SHIFT) +**CLICK** to select multiple files or folders that appear next to each other in the window
- Use (CTRL) +**CLICK** to select multiple files or folders that do not appear next to each other in the window

---

IN ADDITION FINDING A FILE

If you want to locate and select a file but can't remember where it is stored, you use the Find utility on the Start menu. Figure 3.3 shows the results of the Find command for all files beginning with the letter "C" on the Advantage Diskette. To use the Find command, do the following:

1. START: Find, Files or Folders

2. TYPE: *the desired filename,* or *the first few characters and a wild-card (? or *), of the file you are searching for*

3. Specify the search scope using the *Look in* drop-down list box.

4. CLICK: Find Now command button to initiate the search

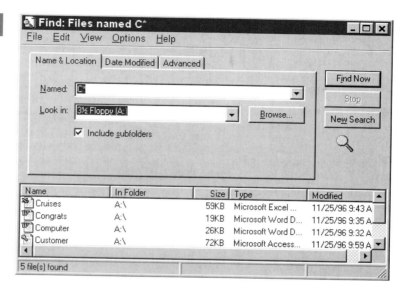

CUSTOMIZING THE VIEW

Using the Menu bar or the shortcut menu, you can customize a window's display to view files using one of the following modes: Large Icons, Small Icons, List, and Details. You can also rearrange the files and folders displayed in a window. In this section, you practice manipulating the appearance of the Advantage Diskette's contents.

Perform the following steps . . .

1. Ensure that the contents of the Advantage Diskette are displayed using large icons in a maximized window.

2. To change the view to Small Icons using the shortcut menu:
   RIGHT-CLICK: *an empty part of the window*
   CHOOSE: View, Small Icons

3. To change to List view:
   RIGHT-CLICK: *an empty part of the window*
   CHOOSE: View, List

4. To change to Details view:
   RIGHT-CLICK: *an empty part of the window*
   CHOOSE: View, Details
   In this view mode, each file's information—size, data type, date of last modification, and attributes—appears in a single row. Your screen should now appear similar to Figure 3.4.

FIGURE 3.4

DISPLAYING FILES IN
DETAILS VIEW MODE

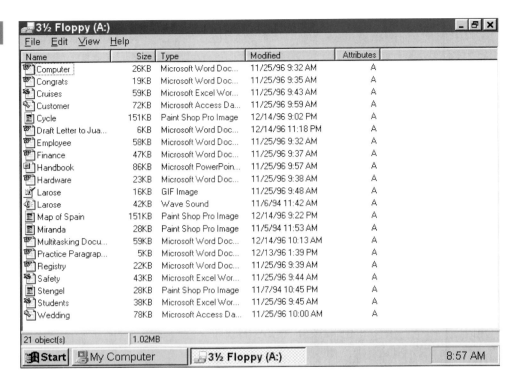

5. To sort the files by their size on the diskette:
   CLICK: Size button located underneath the Menu bar
   Notice that the files are sorted in ascending order, according to their file size.

6. To sort the files in descending order by file size:
   CLICK: Size button again
   (*Note*: This method of clicking the column heading button once for an ascending sort order and twice for a descending sort order is the only method for sorting files in descending order.)

7. You can also change the order of files using a menu command. Do the following to sort the files in the order they were created or last modified:
   RIGHT-CLICK: *an empty part of the window*
   CHOOSE: Arrange Icons, by Date

8. On your own, sort the files in the window by name and then by size.

9. To change the view back to Large Icons:
   RIGHT-CLICK: *an empty part of the window*
   CHOOSE: View, Large Icons

10. For each window you open, "My Computer" remembers the view settings you last specified. Before proceeding:
    CLICK: Close button ([×]) of all open windows
    No windows should appear on the desktop.

QUICK REFERENCE	⏺ From a shortcut menu:
Changing the Appearance of Icons	**RIGHT-CLICK:** *an empty part of the window*
	CHOOSE: View, *an appearance option*
	⏺ From the Menu bar:
	CHOOSE: View, *an appearance option*

QUICK REFERENCE	⏺ From a shortcut menu:
Changing the Sort Order of Icons	**RIGHT-CLICK:** *an empty part of the window*
	CHOOSE: Arrange Icons, *an arrangement option*
	⏺ From the Menu bar:
	CHOOSE: View, Arrange Icons, *an arrangement option*

COPYING AND MOVING FILES

The fastest method for copying and moving files is to use **drag and drop.** Using a mouse, you copy and move files by dragging them from one location to another location (for example, a different folder or disk). Several procedures for using drag and drop are detailed in Table 3.2. An alternative method to drag and drop is to use the Copy, Cut, and Paste commands accessed from the Edit pull-down menu.

TABLE 3.2	*To do this . . .*	*Perform this action . . .*
Drag and Drop Methods for Copying and Moving Files	Move a file from one folder to another folder on the same disk	DRAG: a file icon from one folder to another folder
	Move a file from one disk to another disk	PRESS: (SHIFT) and hold it down DRAG: a file icon from one disk to another disk
	Copy a file from one folder to another folder on the same disk	PRESS: (CTRL) and hold it down DRAG: a file icon from one folder to another folder
	Copy a file from one disk to another disk	DRAG: a file icon from one disk to another disk

In the following exercise, you create a new folder on the Advantage Diskette and then practice using drag and drop to copy and move files.

Perform the following steps . . .

1. Ensure that the Advantage Diskette is in drive A:.

2. DOUBLE-CLICK: "My Computer" icon (🖥) on the desktop
   DOUBLE-CLICK: 🖫 3½ Floppy drive (A:)

3. To create a new folder (called a subdirectory in earlier versions of Windows and Windows NT):
CHOOSE: File, New, Folder
A folder icon appears in the window with its name selected.

4. To name the new folder:
TYPE: Business
PRESS: (ENTER)
Voila! You've created a new folder on the Advantage Diskette. You will work more with folders later in this session.

5. To open the new folder and display its contents:
DOUBLE-CLICK: Business folder icon

6. In this step, you minimize the "My Computer" window so that you can tile the remaining open windows. Do the following:
RIGHT-CLICK: "My Computer" button on the taskbar
CHOOSE: Minimize
(*Note*: You can also click the Minimize button (▬) to minimize the "My Computer" window.)

7. To tile the two open windows:
RIGHT-CLICK: *a blank area on the taskbar*
CHOOSE: Tile Windows Vertically
Your screen should now appear similar to Figure 3.5.

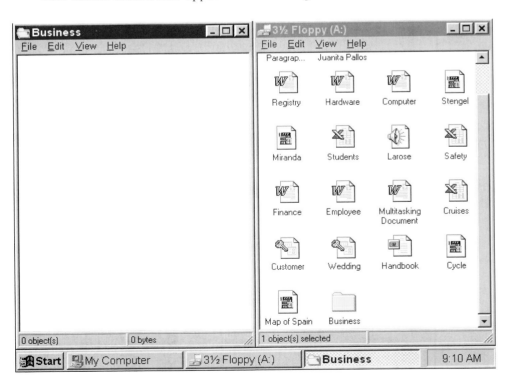

FIGURE 3.5

BUSINESS FOLDER AND
ADVANTAGE DISKETTE
WINDOWS TILED ON
THE DESKTOP

8. To move several files from the root directory of the Advantage Diskette to the Business folder (also on the Advantage Diskette), you must select the files you want to copy. To make this step easier, let's customize the view:
RIGHT-CLICK: *an empty part of the Advantage Diskette window*
CHOOSE: View, Small Icons

9. CLICK: Employee file icon
PRESS: CTRL and hold it down
CLICK: Students file icon
CLICK: Finance file icon

10. Release the CTRL key. The selected files remain highlighted.

11. Position the mouse pointer over one of the highlighted files.

12. CLICK: left mouse button and hold it down
DRAG: mouse pointer to the Business folder window
You will see outlines of the files moving with your pointer as you drag the mouse. To avoid confusion, ignore these outlines and concentrate on positioning the mouse pointer itself on the target folder.

13. When positioned properly over the window, release the mouse button. You will hear the diskette drive and see an animated dialog box with the Title bar "Moving" as the files are moved to their new location.
(*Hint*: If you make a mistake, you can reverse the last drag and drop operation by choosing the Edit, Undo command from the Menu bar of either window.)

14. To make a copy of the Finance file in the same folder:
CLICK: Finance file icon in the Business folder
PRESS: CTRL and hold it down
DRAG: Finance icon to a blank area in the Business folder window
Notice that the icon that you drag has a "plus" sign (+) attached to its outline. This plus sign informs you that you are copying the file.

15. Release the mouse button and then the CTRL key. A file named "Copy of FINANCE" should now appear in the window.

QUICK REFERENCE
Copying Files Using
Drag and Drop

- **To copy selected files to a different disk:**
  DRAG: the desired files between the disks using the mouse
- **To copy selected files on the same disk:**
  PRESS: CTRL **and hold it down, and then DRAG: the files using the mouse**

QUICK REFERENCE
Moving Files Using
Drag and Drop

- **To move selected files to a different disk:**
  PRESS: SHIFT **and hold it down, and then**
  DRAG: the files between the disks using the mouse
- **To move selected files on the same disk:**
  DRAG: the files between the folders using the mouse

RENAMING A FILE

To rename a file, you click on its name once and then, after a short pause, click the name again. Make sure that you do not double-click the name. As an alternative, you can also choose File, Rename from the Menu bar or select the file and press the **F2** function key.

In this exercise, you practice renaming documents that appear in the open windows.

Perform the following steps . . .

1. CLICK: Students filename in the Business folder

2. After a short pause:
   CLICK: Students filename again (not the icon)
   A box appears around the filename and the filename is highlighted.

3. To rename the file:
   TYPE: Student Listing

4. CLICK: *a blank area in the window* to remove the selection box

5. To rename a file using the shortcut menu:
   RIGHT-CLICK: Copy of FINANCE file icon in the Business folder
   CHOOSE: Rename

6. TYPE: Finance Backup
   PRESS: **ENTER**

QUICK REFERENCE
Renaming a File

1. **RIGHT-CLICK:** *the folder icon or filename* that you want to modify
2. **CHOOSE:** Rename
3. **TYPE:** *a new name*
4. **PRESS:** **ENTER**

DELETING A FILE

To delete a file, you click on it once and press the **DELETE** key or drag it to the "Recycle Bin" icon ( ) on the desktop. If you prefer to use menus, you can right-click a file's icon and then choose the Delete command from its shortcut menu. Before actually removing your file, Windows NT asks you for confirmation using a dialog box. You confirm each deletion by clicking the Yes command button.

Any file you delete from the hard disk goes straight to the Recycle Bin, where it sits until you either empty the bin or NT flushes it to make room for more deleted files. Before this happens, you can remove a file from the bin to use it again (i.e. recycle it). You can tell whether the Recycle Bin contains files by the change in its icon graphic to show papers in the bin (for example,   for no deleted files and   for deleted files).

Caution! **Files that you delete from a floppy diskette are not placed into the Recycle Bin.**

Let's practice deleting a file from the Advantage Diskette.

Perform the following steps . . .

1. CLICK: Congrats file icon in the Advantage Diskette window
   PRESS: [DELETE]
   CLICK: Yes button to proceed with the deletion
   The file is removed from the Advantage Diskette. Because you deleted a file from a diskette, the file isn't placed into the Recycle Bin.

2. Let's copy a file to the hard disk (drive C:) and then delete it, so you can see the Recycle Bin in action. Do the following:
   CLICK: "My Computer" button on the taskbar
   DOUBLE-CLICK: ▭◢ drive C: icon
   The root directory of drive C: appears in a window.

3. To straighten up the desktop:
   RIGHT-CLICK: Business button on the taskbar
   CHOOSE: Minimize
   RIGHT-CLICK: "My Computer" button on the taskbar
   CHOOSE: Minimize
   RIGHT-CLICK: *an empty area on the taskbar*
   CHOOSE: Tile Windows Horizontally

4. To change the view of the Advantage Diskette window:
   CLICK: 3½ Floppy (A:) button on the taskbar
   CHOOSE: View, Large Icons
   CHOOSE: View, Arrange Icons, by Name

5. To copy the Cruises file from the Advantage Diskette to the root directory of drive C:, do the following:
   DRAG: Cruises file icon to a blank area in the drive C: window
   The file is copied to the root directory of the hard disk.

   (*CAUTION*: Do not drag and drop the file icon onto a folder in the drive C: window or the file will be copied into the folder.)

6. To change the view of the drive C: window:
   CLICK: drive C: button on the taskbar
   CHOOSE: View, List
   CHOOSE: View, Arrange Icons, by Name
   Your screen should now appear similar, but not identical, to Figure 3.6.

FIGURE 3.6

COPYING A FILE
BETWEEN DISK DRIVES

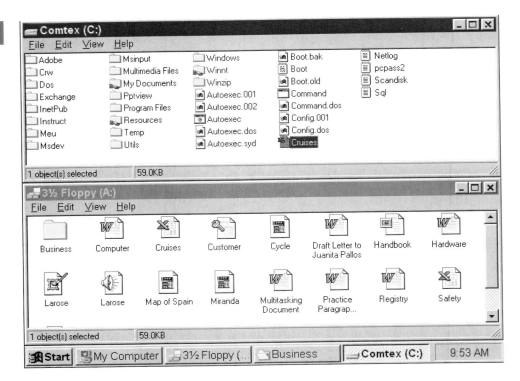

7. Use the vertical scroll bar or rearrange the icons in the window so that you can see the Cruises file icon, as shown in Figure 3.6. Now, let's delete the file from the hard disk. Do the following:
CLICK: Cruises file icon in the drive C: window
PRESS: (DELETE)
CLICK: Yes button to proceed with deleting the file and placing it into the Recycle Bin

8. To view the "Recycle Bin" icon (🗑):
RIGHT-CLICK: *a blank area on the toolbar*
CHOOSE: Minimize All Windows
Notice that the Recycle Bin icon depicts papers in the bin.

9. To open the Recycle Bin:
DOUBLE-CLICK: "Recycle Bin" icon (🗑)
The deleted file appears (as may others on your screen) in the Recycle Bin window.

10. Using the sizing corner on the Recycle Bin window, enlarge the dimensions in order to see the entire entry for the deleted CRUISES file, as shown in Figure 3.7.

FIGURE 3.7

THE RECYCLE
BIN WINDOW

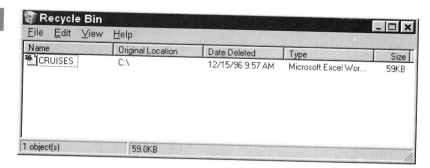

At this point, you can delete the file permanently by selecting it in the Recycle Bin window and pressing **DELETE** or by choosing the File, Empty Recycle Bin command. You can also restore the file to its original location by dragging the file from the Recycle Bin window to a storage location, such as the Advantage Diskette. To reverse the last delete command, choose Edit, Undo Delete from the Menu bar.

11. To permanently delete the Cruises file from the Recycle Bin:
CHOOSE: File, Empty Recycle Bin
CLICK: Yes button to proceed with the deletion
The window should now appear empty.

12. To close the Recycle Bin window:
CLICK: Close button (**✕**)

13. To close the remaining windows without having to open them first, right-click each button on the taskbar and choose the Close command.

QUICK REFERENCE
Deleting a File

1. **SELECT:** *the file or files that you want to delete*
2. **PRESS:** **DELETE**
3. **CLICK:** Yes button in the dialog box

QUICK REFERENCE
Using the
Recycle Bin

1. **DOUBLE-CLICK:** "Recycle Bin" icon (🗑) on the desktop
2. **To restore a file to its original location:**
   RIGHT-CLICK: *the desired file or selected files*
   CHOOSE: Restore from the shortcut menu
3. **To permanently delete a file:**
   RIGHT-CLICK: *the desired file or selected files*
   CHOOSE: Delete from the shortcut menu
4. **To permanently delete all the files in the Recycle Bin:**
   CHOOSE: File, Empty Recycle Bin from the Menu bar

USING UNDO

When managing your folders and files, you may accidentally choose a command with the wrong file selected or simply issue the wrong command altogether. For example, you may move a file to the wrong folder or to the wrong disk. In cases like these, you can choose the Edit, Undo command from the window's Menu bar immediately after making a mistake to reverse the last command or action you performed.

QUICK REFERENCE Using Undo	**Immediately after making a mistake, do the following:** **CHOOSE: Edit, Undo from the Menu bar**

CREATING SHORTCUTS

What is the real purpose of a desktop? For most people, the desktop provides a place to put the tools and documents that need to be accessed most frequently. For example, instead of putting the stapler that you use daily on top of your bookshelf, you might find it more accessible on top of your desk. The Windows NT desktop should be used in a similar fashion. If you often use a particular file, such as a WordPad document, you should consider creating a shortcut to the file and placing that shortcut on the Windows NT desktop.

Shortcuts are pointers to files that let you quickly launch a program or open a document. A shortcut is not a complete copy of a file, it is only a pointer to the original file. Therefore, do not stay awake at night thinking about all your valuable hard disk space lost due to using shortcuts. In this section, you learn how easy it is to create and use shortcuts.

Perform the following steps . . .

1. Ensure that the Advantage Diskette is in drive A: and that the desktop is clear of any open windows.

2. Open the "My Computer" window.

3. Open the 3½ Floppy (A:) window for viewing the contents of the Advantage Diskette.

4. Let's assume that the Registry file is a document that you use quite frequently. To make it faster and easier to access, you will create a shortcut to this document and then place the shortcut directly on the desktop. To begin, position the mouse pointer over the file and do the following:
RIGHT-CLICK: Registry file icon to display a shortcut menu
CHOOSE: Create Shortcut
An icon named "Shortcut to Registry" is created and placed in the 3½ Floppy window. Notice the small shortcut arrow that appears in the bottom left-hand corner of the icon.

5. Before moving this icon to the desktop, let's make some room available:
RIGHT-CLICK: "My Computer" button on the taskbar
CHOOSE: Minimize
If necessary, resize the Advantage Diskette window so that you can see the desktop. Make sure that you scroll the window so that the "Shortcut to Registry" icon is visible.

6. To move this icon to the desktop using drag and drop:
PRESS: (SHIFT) and hold it down
DRAG: Shortcut to Registry icon to the desktop
(*Note*: Remember that you must hold down (SHIFT) to move an icon from one disk to another. In this case, you moved the shortcut icon from the floppy diskette to the desktop stored on drive C:.)

7. Release the mouse button and then (SHIFT).
The shortcut icon now appears on the desktop.

8. To test the shortcut:
DOUBLE-CLICK: Shortcut to Registry icon on the desktop
The document will open into either a WordPad or a Microsoft Word application window, depending on the software that is loaded and registered on your computer.

9. After reading the document, exit WordPad or Microsoft Word:
CHOOSE: File, Exit from the menu

10. If asked to save changes:
CLICK: No

IN ADDITION FILE MANAGEMENT AND CREATING SHORTCUTS USING DRAG AND DROP

By dragging an icon using a right mouse click, you can quickly create shortcuts, and copy and move files or folders. When you release the mouse button, a shortcut menu appears with four commands: Copy Here, Move Here, Create Shortcut(s) Here, and Cancel. Try performing the previous exercise using the right-drag method.

You can rename and delete shortcuts using the same procedures you use for files. When you delete a shortcut from the desktop, the original file isn't affected. That is, it remains stored in its original location on the disk. Let's practice working with shortcuts.

Perform the following steps . . .

1. Minimize the Advantage Diskette window so that there are no open windows on the desktop.

2. To delete the shortcut:
   DRAG: Shortcut to Registry icon to the Recycle Bin using the mouse

3. When the mouse pointer is positioned over the "Recycle Bin" icon ( ), release the mouse button. You should see the icon change to reflect that it now has a deleted file in the bin.

4. To permanently remove the shortcut from the Recycle Bin:
   RIGHT-CLICK: Recycle Bin icon ( )
   CHOOSE: Empty Recycle Bin
   CLICK: Yes command button

5. Close all of the windows that appear on the taskbar before proceeding to the next section.

OTHER FILE-MANAGEMENT COMMANDS

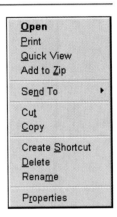

After you select a file in a window, the shortcut menu and File pull-down menu are dynamically modified. Without a file or folder selection in a window, these menus provide a limited set of commands. In the last few sections, you've learned to use the shortcut menu to create a shortcut icon on the desktop, delete a file, and rename a file. In this section, you learn to use some additional commands on the shortcut menu (see the graphic provided) and the File pull-down menu.

Some examples of these commands include:

- *Open*   Opens the selected document using its source application.

- *Print*   Opens the selected document and executes the Print command.

- *Quick View*   Lets you preview a file even if you don't have the source application stored on your computer.

- *Send To*   Lets you direct your files to a diskette, to an electronic mail address, or to the World Wide Web.

- *Properties*   Displays the following about the selected file: (a) its source application, (b) its storage location, and (c) when it was created, last modified, or last accessed.

Although not mentioned in our discussions of "My Computer," you can display a toolbar with shortcut buttons to the tasks explained in this session. From any window, choose the View, Toolbar command. An example of the resulting toolbar appears below:

On your own, display the toolbar for the "My Computer" window on your computer and then position the mouse pointer over a toolbar button. After a moment, a yellow ToolTip will appear with the button's name. You can click a button on the toolbar to perform a task rather than accessing a shortcut menu or the Menu bar.

USING "MY COMPUTER" TO MANAGE DISKS AND FOLDERS

Already in this session, you have created a folder called "Business" on the Advantage Diskette. In this section, you learn more about using "My Computer" to create, manage, and remove folders on a disk. For novice users, "My Computer" is the preferred method for managing the storage areas in your computer. For intermediate to advanced users, the Windows NT Explorer, explained later in this session, provides a more powerful and customizable solution.

CREATING A FOLDER

You create folders to help you better organize your work. For example, you may have one folder dedicated to an important client's documents, another folder for your faxes and memos, and individual folders for each course you are taking at school. Before creating a new folder, you open the "My Computer" window and then select the disk drive where you want the folder to be permanently stored. Once this is done, you create the folder by choosing the New command from the File option on the Menu bar or from a shortcut menu.

Let's practice creating folders on the Advantage Diskette.

Perform the following steps . . .

1. Ensure that the Advantage Diskette is in drive A:.

2. Open the "My Computer" window.

3. Open the 3½ Floppy (A:) window for viewing the contents of the Advantage Diskette.

4. Using the sizing corner, resize the drive A: window to cover a larger portion of the desktop.

5. Make sure that the folders and files are displayed in the Advantage Diskette window using the Large Icons view option. Do the following:
RIGHT-CLICK: *an empty part of the window*
CHOOSE: View, Large Icons
RIGHT-CLICK: *an empty part of the window*
CHOOSE: Arrange Icons, by Name

6. To create a new folder called Word Data:
RIGHT-CLICK: *an empty part of the window*
CHOOSE: New, Folder
A folder entitled "New Folder" appears on the desktop. (*Note*: If you want to use the File, New command from the Menu bar, make sure that there are no files selected in the window before issuing the command.)

7. Since the folder's title is already highlighted, you can simply type over the name to create your new folder. Do the following:
TYPE: Word Data
PRESS: (ENTER)

8. To create a new folder called Excel Data:
RIGHT-CLICK: *an empty part of the window*
CHOOSE: New, Folder
TYPE: Excel Data
PRESS: (ENTER)

9. In Windows, folders can contain folders. To create two folders—named Letters and Memos, respectively—inside the Word Data folder, you first open the Word Data folder.
DOUBLE-CLICK: Word Data folder icon

10. To create the Letters folder:
RIGHT-CLICK: *an empty part of the Word Data window*
CHOOSE: New, Folder
TYPE: Letters
PRESS: (ENTER)

11. To create the Memos folder:
RIGHT-CLICK: *an empty part of the Word Data window*
CHOOSE: New, Folder
TYPE: Memos
PRESS: (ENTER)

12. To arrange the icons in the Word Data folder:
RIGHT-CLICK: *an empty part of the Word Data window*
CHOOSE: Arrange Icons, Auto Arrange

13. Close the Word Data window.

14. RIGHT-CLICK: *an empty part of the drive A: window*
CHOOSE: Arrange Icons, by Name
Your screen should now look similar to Figure 3.8.

FIGURE 3.8

CREATING NEW FOLDERS

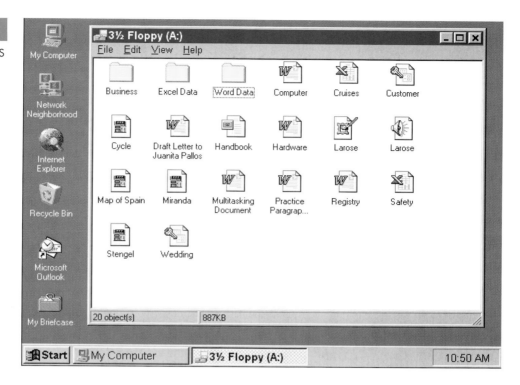

QUICK REFERENCE

Creating a Folder

1. **Open the disk or folder where you want to create the new folder.**
2. **RIGHT-CLICK:** *an empty part of the window*
3. **CHOOSE: New, Folder from the shortcut menu**
4. **TYPE:** *a folder name*

COPYING FILES INTO A FOLDER

In this section, you practice moving files into the new folders on the Advantage Diskette. The general process is identical to that described earlier in this session. When moving and copying files among folders, the majority of the steps involve preparing the desktop by opening and organizing the appropriate windows. The actual act of moving or copying involves a simple drag and drop operation.

In the following steps, you will move—using drag and drop—all the WordPad documents () from the root directory of the Advantage Diskette (3½ Floppy window) into the Letters folder that is located inside the Word Data folder.

Perform the following steps . . .

1. If you completed the last section, the Advantage Diskette window (3½ Floppy) should appear on the screen.

2. To open the Letters folder of the Word Data folder:
DOUBLE-CLICK: Word Data folder icon
DOUBLE-CLICK: Letters folder icon

3. To make room on the desktop for the move operation, minimize the Word Data and "My Computer" windows using the following process:
RIGHT-CLICK: Word Data button on the taskbar
CHOOSE: Minimize
RIGHT-CLICK: "My Computer" button on the taskbar
CHOOSE: Minimize

4. To tile the two open windows:
RIGHT-CLICK: *an empty area on the taskbar*
CHOOSE: Tile Windows Vertically

5. To see all the icons in the Advantage Diskette window (3½ Floppy):
RIGHT-CLICK: *an empty part of the window*
CHOOSE: View, Small Icons
RIGHT-CLICK: *an empty part of the window*
CHOOSE: Arrange Icons, Auto Arrange

6. To make the process of selecting all of the WordPad and Microsoft Word files easier, sort the files in the Advantage Diskette window by file type:
RIGHT-CLICK: *an empty part of the window*
CHOOSE: Arrange Icons, by Type

7. To select the WordPad or Microsoft Word files, click the first document in the list. Hold down the (SHIFT) key and then click the last WordPad or Microsoft Word document. Before continuing, all WordPad and Microsoft Word documents should be selected in the Advantage Diskette window. You can then release the (SHIFT) key. You may also want to use the (CTRL) +CLICK combination to select files.

Your screen should now look similar to Figure 3.9. (*Note*: A different number of files may be displaying on your Advantage Diskette.)

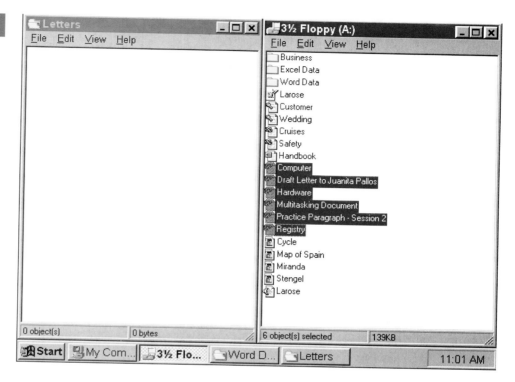

8. To move the selected files to the Letters folder, position the mouse pointer over one of the highlighted files and then do the following:
DRAG: mouse pointer and file icons to the Letters folder window

9. Release the mouse button. The files are moved to the Letters folder.

10. To organize the icons in the Letters folder:
RIGHT-CLICK: *an empty part of the window*
CHOOSE: Arrange Icons, Auto Arrange

11. Close the Letters folder.

12. On your own, move the Excel files (⬛) from the Advantage Diskette window (3½ Floppy) to the Excel Data folder.

RENAMING A FOLDER

Renaming a folder is the same as renaming a file. To rename a folder, you click on its name once and then, after a short pause, click the name again. You can also right-click the file and choose Rename from its shortcut menu or choose the File, Rename command from the Menu bar. In this section, you practice renaming the folders that you created earlier.

Perform the following steps . . .

1. CLICK: Business folder name

2. After a short pause:
   CLICK: Business folder name again (not the icon)
   A box appears around the filename and the filename is highlighted.

3. To rename the file:
   TYPE: Working Papers
   PRESS: [ENTER]

4. CLICK: *a blank area in the window* to remove the selection box

REMOVING A FOLDER

"My Computer" provides three methods for removing a folder. Each procedure requires that you first select the folder you want to remove. To remove a selected folder, you can press [DELETE] or choose Delete from the shortcut menu. You can also choose the Delete command from the File pull-down menu. If you choose to remove a folder that contains files, Windows displays a dialog box confirming that you want to delete the files. (*Note*: To move a folder to another disk or folder, choose Edit, Cut from the Menu bar, move to the desired destination, and then choose Edit, Paste.)

Let's practice removing folders using "My Computer."

Perform the following steps . . .

1. CLICK: Working Papers folder

2. PRESS: [DELETE]

3. To proceed with removing the Working Papers folder:
   CLICK: Yes button to proceed
   The folder and all its contents are deleted permanently; since it was on the diskette, it is not sent to the Recycle Bin.

4. Before proceeding, close all the open windows so that only the Start button appears on the taskbar.

QUICK REFERENCE
Removing a Folder

- **CLICK:** *the folder name*
- **PRESS:** [DELETE]
- **CLICK: Yes command button to proceed with the procedure**

PREPARING NEW DISKETTES

Some new diskettes have to be formatted, or initialized, before you can use them on your computer. However, most diskettes can now be purchased pre-formatted for IBM-compatible computers. You can also format existing diskettes to check the integrity of the diskette, create a new storage structure on the diskette, and remove any existing information.

To format a diskette, you insert the diskette into the diskette drive and, from the "My Computer" window, right-click the icon that represents the drive and choose the Format command. Windows NT lets you choose from various formatting options. With fixed disks, you can specify the File System to be FAT (File Allocation Table), which is DOS-compatible, or NTFS (NT File System), which is not DOS-compatible. With an NTFS file system, you can also enable compression and change the allocation unit size per sector. The exercises in this guide assume that you are working on a FAT-formatted fixed disk.

QUICK REFERENCE	1.	**RIGHT-CLICK:** *a diskette drive's icon* **to display its shortcut menu**
Formatting a Diskette	2.	**CHOOSE: Format**
	3.	**CHOOSE:** *formatting options* **from the Format dialog box**
	4.	**CLICK: Start command button**

DISPLAYING DISK PROPERTIES

You can display usage and capacity statistics for a hard disk or floppy diskette using the Properties dialog box. After right-clicking a disk icon in the "My Computer" window, choose the Properties command. In addition to reviewing a pie chart of the disk's free and used space, you can change the name or label of the disk from this dialog box.

Let's review the properties of the disks installed in your system.

Perform the following steps . . .

1. Ensure that the Advantage Diskette is in drive A:.

2. Open the "My Computer" window.

3. RIGHT-CLICK: 3½ Floppy (A:) icon for the Advantage Diskette
   CHOOSE: Properties

4. To enter a volume name for the diskette:
   CLICK: *General* tab
   TYPE: Advantage
   Your screen should appear similar, but not identical, to Figure 3.10.

5. After you are finished viewing the dialog box:
   CLICK: OK or PRESS: (ENTER)

6. Close the "My Computer" window before proceeding to the next section.

FIGURE 3.10

DISPLAYING DISK
PROPERTIES

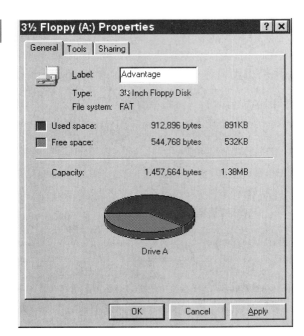

3½ Floppy (A:) Properties

General | Tools | Sharing |

Label: Advantage

Type: 3½ Inch Floppy Disk
File system: FAT

■ Used space: 912,896 bytes 891KB
■ Free space: 544,768 bytes 532KB

Capacity: 1,457,664 bytes 1.38MB

Drive A

OK   Cancel   Apply

QUICK REFERENCE
Displaying Disk Properties

1. **RIGHT-CLICK:** *a drive's icon* **to display its shortcut menu**
2. **CHOOSE: Properties**
3. **SELECT:** *General* **tab to display usage statistics**
4. **CLICK: OK when finished viewing the dialog box**

IN ADDITION ACCESSING ADDITIONAL DISK UTILITIES

From the *Tools* tab of the Properties dialog box, you can choose to check the disk for errors, back up the disk's information, or *defragment* the disk. A disk becomes

fragmented when its individual files are stored in pieces around the disk. Defragmenting a disk improves its performance by bringing these pieces together.

USING WINDOWS NT EXPLORER

Now that you've had experience managing files and disks using "My Computer," you will find it easier to learn and use the Windows NT Explorer. As we mentioned at the beginning of this session, "My Computer" is the easier file-management model for beginners to use, whereas NT Explorer is preferred by intermediate to experienced users. Now, let's explain why.

By default, "My Computer" displays a separate window for every disk and folder you open. To display the contents of a single folder on a disk, for example, you typically open three windows: (1) the "My Computer" window, (2) a window displaying the contents of the disk, and (3) a window displaying the contents of the folder. To copy a file from a folder on one disk to a folder on another disk, you can easily have five windows open at a given time. Although the "My Computer" model hides the concept of hierarchies and is intuitive for first-time users, it clutters your work area and makes inefficient use of the desktop. As you may have noticed in this session, we have spent a fair amount of time minimizing, tiling, and closing windows.

You have two options for dealing with this overcrowding of the desktop. First, you can change the Windows default of opening a new window each time you double-click an object. To do so, choose the View, Options command from the "My Computer" window's Menu bar. On the *Folder* tab, you would then select the *Browse folders by using a single window that changes as you open each folder* option button and click the OK command button. As you double-click folders, the current window's icons are replaced by the selected folder's icons. To move back up one level in the hierarchy, you press the (BACKSPACE) key. A second and more preferable alternative is to use the Windows NT Explorer. The NT Explorer provides single-step access to all the resources on your computer, including disks, folders, printers, and other devices. The next section provides a guided tour of NT Explorer.

THE NT EXPLORER WINDOW

To load NT Explorer, you choose the Programs, Windows NT Explorer command from the Start menu. If you are already working in the "My Computer" window, you can right-click a drive icon and then choose Explore from its shortcut menu. When NT Explorer is first loaded, your computer's resources, including disk drives, are displayed in the left pane of the NT Explorer window and the selected drive's folders and files are displayed in the right pane (Figure 3.11). If you want to manage a different drive, you select the desired drive in the left pane of the current window or you can open a new NT Explorer window. You can also move, size, and arrange multiple NT Explorer windows on the desktop to best suit your needs and available work space.

FIGURE 3.11

THE WINDOWS
NT EXPLORER

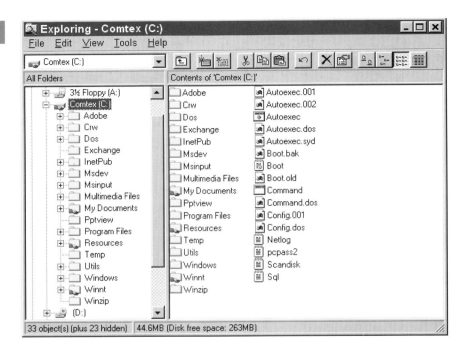

The NT Explorer window is divided into two panes by a vertical line called the **Split bar.** You can use the Split bar to increase or decrease the viewing area for either pane. The right pane shows the contents of the selected resource or disk in the left pane. The left pane in the NT Explorer window shows your computer's resources and disk drive hierarchies using an outline format that you can collapse and expand. You may notice the appearance of plus and minus signs beside names in the left pane. If a resource or folder contains additional items that aren't displaying in the pane, a plus sign (+) appears to the left of its name. You click the plus sign to expand the detail displayed. A minus sign (-) indicates that all the items are currently displayed. If there is no plus or minus sign displayed next to a name, you can immediately determine that there are no additional items contained in the resource or folder to display.

Let's load the Windows NT Explorer using the shortcut menu.

Perform the following steps . . .

1. Ensure that the Advantage Diskette is in drive A:.

2. Open the "My Computer" window.

3. To load NT Explorer and view the contents of drive C:, do the following:
   RIGHT-CLICK: drive C: icon to display its shortcut menu
   CHOOSE: Explore

4. Maximize the NT Explorer window before continuing.

QUICK REFERENCE
Loading NT
Explorer

- **From the "My Computer" window:**
  RIGHT-CLICK: *a drive icon* **to display its shortcut menu**
  CHOOSE: Explore
- **Using the Start button on the taskbar:**
  START: Programs, Windows NT Explorer

PUTTING NT EXPLORER TO WORK

Most of the file-management procedures you used in "My Computer" work similarly in Windows NT Explorer, including selecting folders and files, customizing the view, copying and moving files, renaming and deleting files, using Undo, creating and removing folders, and creating shortcuts. You can also access the shortcut menu of a folder or file using the right-click approach.

In this section, you practice using the NT Explorer window to display the contents of your disks and to perform some simple file-management tasks.

Perform the following steps . . .

1. Ensure that the Advantage Diskette is in drive A: and that the NT Explorer window is maximized.

2. DRAG: the left pane's vertical scroll bar to the top of the Split Pane
   Notice that "Desktop" appears at the top of the hierarchy.

3. DOUBLE-CLICK: ⊞ Desktop icon
   Right now, you're looking at an aerial photo of your computer system in the right pane. You should also note the title Contents of 'Desktop' which appears above the right pane.

4. To zoom in for some more detail:
   DOUBLE-CLICK: ⊞ Desktop icon in the left pane
   DOUBLE-CLICK: ⊞ 3½ Floppy (A:) in the left pane
   The contents of the root directory of the Advantage Diskette appear in the right pane. By double-clicking the icon, you selected the drive for viewing and expanded the folder structure below the icon.

5. To zoom in even further:
   CLICK: Excel Data folder in the left pane
   The contents of the Excel Data folder now appear in the right pane. Notice that only one window is displaying on the desktop. In "My Computer," you would typically display three windows before displaying the contents of the Excel Data folder.

6. Let's create a new folder on the Advantage Diskette using NT Explorer:
CLICK: 3½ Floppy drive (A:) in the left pane
RIGHT-CLICK: *an empty area in the right pane*
CHOOSE: New, Folder from the shortcut menu
TYPE: `Access Data`
PRESS: ENTER
Notice that the Access Data folder appears in both panes.

7. Let's move some files from the root directory of the Advantage Diskette to the new folder. Do the following:
CLICK: Wedding
PRESS: CTRL and hold it down
CLICK: Customer

8. Release the CTRL key and then position the mouse pointer over one of the highlighted files.

9. DRAG: selected files over the Access Data folder in the left pane until the folder's name appears highlighted

10. Release the mouse button to complete the move operation.

11. To view the contents of the new folder:
CLICK: Access Data folder in the left pane
You should see the two files appear in the right pane.

12. To return one level higher in the structure:
CLICK: 3½ Floppy drive (A:) in the left pane
As you can see, the procedures you use in NT Explorer are very similar to the ones you performed with "My Computer" earlier in this session.

SHARING FILES, FOLDERS, AND DISKS

With the inherent networking capabilities of Windows NT, you have the ability to share resources in a network setting. Establishing peer group networking, whereby you share your computer's resources with other users, is a relatively simple process using NT Workstation. For example, you can connect to and share the following resources on an NT network: files, folders, disks, CD-ROM drives, backup devices, removable and optical drives, and printers. This section demonstrates how you, as the administrator of your computer, can specify folders to be shared on the network. (*Note:* Your computer must be turned on for others to access its resources on the network.)

Perform the following steps . . .

1. Ensure that the Advantage Diskette is in drive A: and that the NT Explorer window is maximized.

2. To share the Excel Data folder with other users on your network:
RIGHT-CLICK: Excel Data folder in the left pane
CHOOSE: Sharing
The Excel Data Properties dialog box appears with the *Sharing* tab selected.

3. To share this folder:
   CLICK: *Shared As* option button
   Your screen should now appear similar to Figure 3.12.

FIGURE 3.12

SHARING THE EXCEL
DATA FOLDER

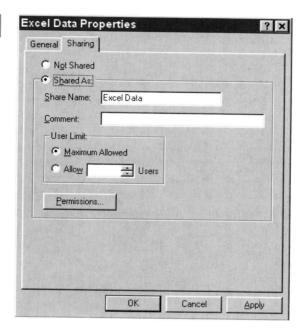

4. For compatibility with DOS and Windows 3.1 users on your network, you should attempt to keep your resource names to eight characters or fewer. Do the following:
   SELECT: the text "Excel Data" in the *Share Name* text box
   TYPE: XLData

5. To set the maximum number of users who can concurrently access your shared resource:
   CLICK: *Allow* option button
   The number "10" should appear automatically in the Spin box. This number is not random; it follows the NT Workstation license, which allows up to ten users to connect to your computer.

6. To specify what the users are allowed to do with the XLData folder:
   CLICK: Permissions command button
   You are now presented with a dialog box for selecting users and assigning rights and permissions.

7. To specify the type of access permission:
   CLICK: down arrow adjacent to the *Type of Access* drop-down list box
   Your screen should appear similar to Figure 3.13. In this list box, you can specify whether your users have permission to read the information only, read and update the information, or read, update, and delete the information in the XLData folder.

FIGURE 3.13

SPECIFYING SHARE
PERMISSIONS

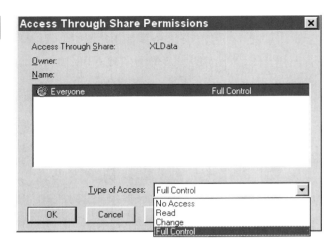

8. SELECT: Full Control in the *Type of Access* drop-down list box
CLICK: OK command button

9. To accept your choices and begin sharing the folder:
CLICK: OK command button
When you return to the NT Explorer window, you will notice that the icon
has changed from showing a normal folder ⬜ to a shared folder 🖐.
(*CAUTION*: You should use a password and limit access permissions when
sharing a resource on a network!)

10. You will learn more about NT's networking features in the Appendix.
Let's shut down NT Explorer and Windows. Do the following:
CHOOSE: File, Close to exit NT Explorer

11. Close all of the open windows on the desktop.

12. To shut down Windows NT:
START: Shut Down
CLICK: *Shut down the computer?* option button
CLICK: Yes command button

QUICK REFERENCE
Sharing a Storage
Resource

1. **RIGHT-CLICK:** *the desired resource* (i.e., file, folder, or disk)

2. **CHOOSE: Sharing**

3. Select the desired options from the *Sharing* tab of the dialog box.

4. **CLICK: OK command button**

SUMMARY

This session introduced you to two models for managing files and folders: "My Computer" and Windows NT Explorer. After a brief explanation of file- and disk-management basics, the session led you through using "My Computer" to copy, move, rename, and delete files and folders. You were then introduced to Windows NT Explorer, a more advanced management tool that displays your files hierarchically in a dual-paned window. Lastly, you learned how to share a resource from your computer with other users on your network.

COMMAND SUMMARY

Many of the commands and procedures appearing in this session are provided in the command summary in Table 3.3.

TABLE 3.3	Task Description	General Instruction
Command Summary	Select a file or folder	Click the file or folder icon.
	Select more than one file	Click the first file. Press **CTRL** and hold it down while clicking additional files. If the files are contiguous, you may **SHIFT**+CLICK to select a group of files.
	Change the appearance of icons	Right-click an empty part of a window and choose View, *an appearance option* from the menu.
	Change the order of icons	Right-click an empty part of a window and choose View, *an arrangement option* from the menu.
	Copy or move a file selection	Select the files to move or copy. Drag the files between disk drives (copy) or directories (move). You can also use the **CTRL** and **SHIFT** keys to change the functionality of drag and drop.
	Rename a file	Click the filename once. After a short pause, click the filename again. Type the new filename.
	Delete a file selection	Select the desired file(s) and then press **DELETE**. You can also right-click a file and then choose Delete from its shortcut menu.
	Open the Recycle Bin	Double-click the "Recycle Bin" icon (🗑) on the desktop to view the files in the Recycle Bin. Use options on the Menu bar to restore deleted files or permanently delete the files.

	Task Description	*General Instruction*
TABLE 3.3 ***Continued***	Reverse file operations	Choose Edit, Undo from the Menu bar to reverse the last command executed.
	Create a file shortcut	Right-click the file to display its shortcut menu. Choose the Create Shortcut command. Drag the shortcut to the desktop. You can also right-drag a file to copy the file, move the file, or create a shortcut for the file.
	Create a folder	Open the disk or folder where you want to create a new folder. Right-click an empty area of the window to display its shortcut menu. Choose the New, Folder command. Type a folder name.
	Remove a folder	Select the folder and then press **DELETE**. You can also right-click a folder and then choose Delete from its shortcut menu.
	Format a diskette	Right-click a drive's icon to display its shortcut menu. Click Format and then the Start button.
	Loading NT Explorer	Choose Programs, Windows NT Explorer from the Start menu. You can also right-click a resource and then choose the Explore command.
	Share a file, folder, or disk with other users	Right-click the desired item in the "My Computer" window or NT Explorer window and choose the Sharing command from the shortcut menu.

 **K**EY TERMS

data files

Disk files that contain work created or entered using an application program that is not recognized by Windows.

document files

Disk files that contain work created or entered using an application program recognized by Windows.

drag and drop

The ability to copy and move files by selecting them and then dragging them to a different disk location.

folder

A folder is a special type of file that is used to store and organize other program, document, and data files.

program files

Disk files that contain instructions for the CPU to perform specific tasks or operations.

root directory

The directory that is created when you format a disk. Folders are created from the root directory, which is the uppermost level in the hierarchy.

shortcut

A pointer to a file, folder, drive, or other resource on your computer system. A shortcut is not a complete copy of a resource, it is only a pointer to the original resource.

Split bar

The vertical line that separates the left pane of the NT Explorer window from the right pane. You can adjust the size of either pane by dragging the Split bar.

EXERCISES

SHORT ANSWER

1. What are the three categories of files that appear on hard disks and floppy disks? Define each category.

2. Name the directory where files are stored on a newly formatted disk.

3. Explain why folders are important to disk management.

4. Summarize the rules for naming files using Windows NT.

5. Explain two methods for selecting more than one file in a window.

6. What does a + (plus sign) signify in the left pane of the NT Explorer?

7. What is the purpose of the Find command?

8. What does it mean to "format" a disk?

9. How would you allow the other users on your network to access the CD-ROM drive in your computer?

10. Compare "My Computer" and Windows NT Explorer. How are these two applications different? How are they alike?

HANDS-ON

(*Note*: Ensure that you know the storage location of your Advantage Files and your Data Files before proceeding.)

1. This exercise enables you to practice some of the file-management commands that you used with "My Computer" during this session.

   a. Ensure that the Advantage Diskette is placed into drive A:.

   b. Open the "My Computer" window and then display the contents of the Advantage Diskette.

   c. Size the window to cover a large portion of the desktop.

   d. Arrange the files in order by file type.

e. Display the files showing all details.

f. Display the file list in order by file size.

g. Display the files using large icons.

h. Auto-arrange the icons in the open window.

2. This exercise lets you practice copying, deleting, and renaming files on the Advantage Diskette.

a. Ensure that the files on the Advantage Diskette are displayed in a window.

b. Open the Word Data folder. (*Note:* You created the Word Data folder in this session.)

c. Open the Letters folder.

d. Minimize the Word Data and "My Computer" windows.

e. Tile the two open windows horizontally.

f. Select all the files in the Letters window.

g. Copy all the files to the root directory of the Advantage Diskette.

h. Maximize the Advantage Diskette window.

i. Rename the Hardware file to Hardware Overview.

j. Delete the file named Stengel from the Advantage Diskette.
Your screen should now appear similar, but not identical, to Figure 3.14.

FIGURE 3.14

MANIPULATING A
WINDOW'S CONTENTS

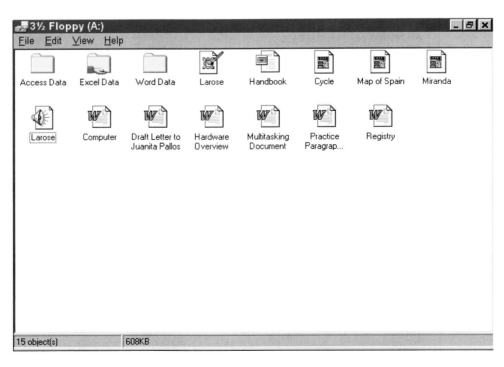

3. In this exercise, you create a folder and then copy files into it.

   a. Ensure that the Advantage Diskette is placed into drive A:.

   b. Close all of the open windows, except for "My Computer" and the Advantage Diskette.

   c. Ensure that both "My Computer" and the Advantage Diskette windows are visible on the desktop.

   d. Tile the two windows vertically.

   e. Create a folder named Multimedia in the root directory of the Advantage Diskette.

   f. Move the following files into the Multimedia folder: Larose (two files) and Miranda.

   g. Arrange the icons in the Multimedia folder.

   h. Close all open windows.

4. In this exercise, you practice launching Windows NT Explorer from the "My Computer" window and issuing file-management commands.

   a. Ensure that the Advantage Diskette is placed into drive A:.

   b. Open the "My Computer" window.

   c. Decrease the size of the window and move it to the top left-hand corner of the screen.

   d. Point to the icon that represents drive A: and launch NT Explorer from its shortcut menu.

   e. Click the "My Computer" button on the taskbar.

   f. Repeat Step c so that two NT Explorer windows are displaying the contents of drive A:.

   g. Minimize the "My Computer" window using the taskbar.

   h. Arrange the two NT Explorer windows so that they appear tiled horizontally on the desktop.

   i. Change the view to a list for both NT Explorer windows.

   j. Copy the file named Hardware Overview into the Multimedia folder. Remember to copy the file, not move it.

   k. Rename the Hardware Overview file, located in the Multimedia folder, to Multimedia Hardware.

   l. Delete the file named Handbook from the root directory of the Advantage Diskette.

   m. Close one of the NT Explorer windows and maximize the other.

   n. Close the remaining NT Explorer window.

5. **On Your Own:** Creating a Shortcut

   a. Use "My Computer" or Windows NT Explorer to create a shortcut to the Multitasking Document that is located in the root directory of the Advantage Diskette.

   b. Place the shortcut on the desktop.

   c. Open the Multitasking Document using the new desktop shortcut.

   d. Exit the application (WordPad/Word) once it has loaded and you've had a chance to review the document.

   e. Delete the shortcut from the desktop.

   f. Close any open windows.

6. **On Your Own:** Creating a Filing Cabinet
   In this exercise, you need to create a series of folders on the Advantage Diskette for the following topics: Recipes and Sports. In the Recipes folder, create three additional folders: Appetizers, Entrees, and Desserts. In the Sports folder, create four additional folders: Baseball, Golf, Swimming, and Tennis. Using WordPad, create a document describing the folder structure under Recipes and then save it to that folder. Then, create a similar document for the Sports folder. Once completed, close all open windows on the desktop and shut down Windows NT.

CASE PROBLEMS   **BERKFORD COLLEGE, PENNSYLVANIA**

(*Note*: In the following case problems, assume the role of the primary characters and perform the same steps that they identify. You may want to reread the session opening.)

1. Sharon Rheingold is on a mission. After several evenings of study at the campus computer lab, she is now comfortable using the Windows accessory programs, "My Computer," and Windows NT Explorer. With the start of classes only a few days away, Sharon is ready to put her first three lectures together using WordPad.

   Her schedule being quite tight this past week, Sharon was only able to jot down the major topic headings for her outlines, as follows:

   Lecture 1: Five Cs for Excellence in Public Speaking
   - *Confident*
   - *Competent*
   - *Credible*
   - *Convincing*
   - *Comfortable*

Lecture 2: Reasons for Experiencing Stage Fright
- *Fear of failure*
- *Lack of confidence*
- *Lack of preparation*
- *Lack of knowledge about topic*
- *Lack of knowledge about audience*

Lecture 3: Methods for Overcoming Stage Fright
- *Be positive*
- *Practice often*
- *Prepare thoroughly*
- *Research your topic*
- *Research your audience*

Now Sharon has to create three separate lecture files, which she calls PS-LEC1, PS-LEC2, and PS-LEC3. Then, she'll save them to her Data Files location. Ensure that you create each lecture as a separate file using WordPad.

2. Completing her first task of creating the first three lectures, Sharon realizes that she has another hour before dinner and so she creates a fourth lecture (as shown below). For this lecture, she decides to use the Windows Notepad program instead of WordPad. She saves the lecture as LECTURE4 onto the Advantage Diskette and then closes Notepad.

Lecture 4: Types of Presentations
- *Technical (for describing technical specifications and terminology)*
- *Instructional (for communicating a process or procedure to learners)*
- *Illustrative (for enhancing understanding with anecdotal stories)*
- *Demonstrative (for enhancing understanding with live demonstration)*
- *Discussion (for conducting relatively informal group meetings)*

3. At noon on the following day, Walt arrives home to find Sharon hunched over the computer. "I thought you finished writing your lecture outlines last night, Sharon." He strolls over to the desk to see what she is working on. Not looking up from the computer, Sharon replies, "Oh yeah, I did. But I realized that I saved my fourth lecture using a different naming format than the first three. I'm using Windows NT Explorer to rename the file from LECTURE4 to PS-LEC4." She completes the job and then leans back in her chair.

"With all of these files, it's going to get harder and harder to manage my work, especially with all the new stuff I'm creating each week." Sharon lets out a deep sigh. Walt looks at the NT Explorer window and then offers the following advice, "What I think you should do is create a folder in your Data Files location called PS101 for all of your Public Speaking 101 course material. And in that folder, I suggest you create additional folders for each week's lecture materials. For example, create WEEK1 and WEEK2 folders in the PS101 folder. Then, you can move your first two lectures into the WEEK1 folder and lectures 3 and 4 into the WEEK2 folder. If you continue managing your work using that system, you'll have an easy time of it!"

Assume the role of Sharon and perform the steps recommended by Walt for managing her first four lecture files.

4.   With her outlines neatly managed and stored away in folders, Sharon decides to perform one last task. On a whim, she had created the fourth lecture using Windows Notepad, but now she wants to convert that outline to the WordPad format of her other lectures. Before jumping onto the computer, Sharon plans out the steps in her mind. First, she will open the PS-LEC4 lecture using Notepad and then copy the outline to the Clipboard. She can then minimize the Notepad program and launch WordPad. After pasting the outline from the Clipboard into WordPad, she will save the file as PS-LEC4 into the WEEK2 subdirectory. She will then close both Notepad and Word-Pad, and then delete the original Notepad PS-LEC4 file.

Perform the steps on your computer that Sharon has outlined above.

Customizing Windows

INTRODUCTION

We all have ideas and preferences about how our desks should be organized. For example, some people like everything to remain in their desk drawers except for the document they're reviewing, while others prefer a cluttered, "lived-in" look. It is natural, therefore, that we have preferences about how we want the Windows NT desktop to look and function. In this session, you learn how to customize Windows NT to the way you work.

THE RIVER REPORT

The *River Report* is a weekly publication that provides news reports, announcements, and general interest stories for the Sacramento River region. Linda James, a graduate of Stanford's journalism program, just accepted the position of editor for the small-town newspaper. In her new position, Linda is responsible for identifying leads, editing articles written by her reporters, and, most importantly, getting the paper out every Friday.

Her new office is well-appointed with a large oak desk and a new Pentium™ computer system. However, her predecessor, Hank Leary, had too great a liking for the 1970s, as exhibited by the orange shag carpet, dark wood paneling, and velvet paintings of Elvis. Linda definitely has some work to do in making the editor's office her own!

Having removed the art from the walls, Linda settles into the leather chair and turns on the computer. After a few seconds, she is greeted by the familiar Windows desktop. "OH MY!" she blurts out. After blinking her eyes several times, she leans forward slowly. "Hank Leary must be color blind," she thinks to herself. The screen beams out a fluorescent color scheme that could easily light up the entire office at night. In addition to the office carpet and paneling, Linda needs to redecorate her Windows desktop! Unfortunately, she has never customized Microsoft Windows NT and doesn't know where to begin.

In this session, you and Linda learn how to customize the Windows desktop by adding files and programs to the Start menu and by choosing color schemes and wallpaper for the background. You also learn how to use the system clock, display regional settings, change the mouse settings, control sounds, install hardware and software, and work with the Printers folder. So turn on your lava lamp and let's get started!

CUSTOMIZING THE START MENU

In an effort to streamline your interaction with windows and icons, Windows NT lets you create shortcuts to the files or programs you use most often. From last session, you will already be familiar with creating and placing a shortcut on the desktop. You now learn how to add shortcuts to the Start menu. You customize the Start menu by choosing Settings, Taskbar from the Start menu or by right-clicking an empty area on the taskbar and then selecting the Properties command.

UNDERSTANDING USER PROFILES

Windows NT allows you to log on to the computer with a unique user name and password. In addition to having security implications, your login name also directs NT where to look for your **user profile.** A user profile is a directory structure that contains your specific configuration options. For example, after you log on to NT, it retrieves your settings for screen colors and appearance, network and printer connections, and program items for the Start menu. This feature allows multiple users to work on the same computer, yet have access to different programs and be able to personalize their desktops. The Administrator controls the assignment of new accounts and profiles.

The **group** that you belong to, whether Administrator, Guest, Power User, or Default User, determines what rights and **permissions** you have and what types of customizing tasks you are able to perform. Figure 4.1 shows the User Manager application, accessed by choosing Programs, Administrative Tools (Common), User Manager from the Start menu. Notice the default groups that have been provided upon installation.

FIGURE 4.1

USER MANAGER
WINDOW

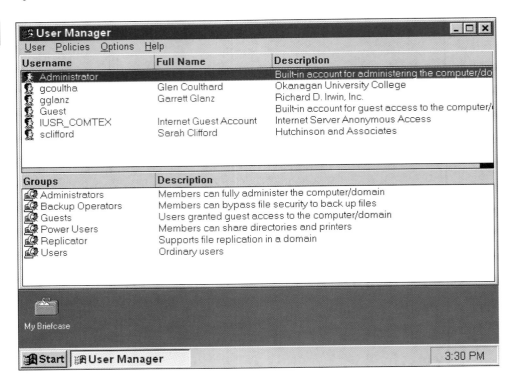

ADDING A DOCUMENT SHORTCUT TO THE START MENU

In this section, you create a shortcut to the document file named "Hardware Overview" that is stored on the Advantage Diskette. You will position the shortcut in the Start menu so that it may be accessed quickly at any time. Although the following instructions refer to the Advantage Diskette, you may have stored your Advantage Files on the local hard drive or a network drive. Ensure that you know the correct location before proceeding.

Perform the following steps . . .

1. Ensure that the Advantage Diskette is in drive A:.

2. Open the "My Computer" window.

3. Open the ⌐ 3½ Floppy (A:) window for viewing the contents of the Advantage Diskette.

4. DRAG: Hardware Overview file icon over the [Start] button (*CAUTION*: Only perform this step once! Do not expect any fireworks or applause from NT for adding this item to the menu. You must proceed to the next few steps to see any results.)

5. Release the mouse button to complete the drag operation.

6. To see what you've accomplished by dragging and dropping an icon: CLICK: [Start] Notice that "Hardware Overview" now appears at the top of the Start menu, as shown in Figure 4.2.

FIGURE 4.2

THE START MENU WITH A NEW MENU OPTION ADDED

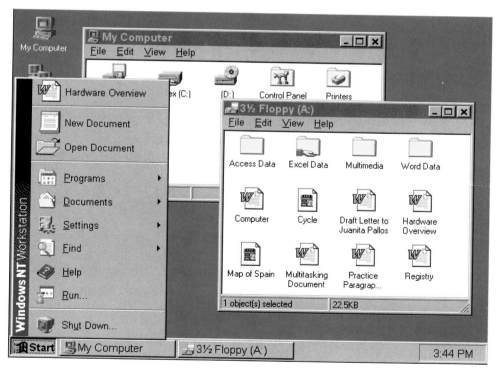

7. To rename the "Hardware Overview" menu item to "Computer Document," do the following: CLICK: *anywhere on the desktop* to remove the Start menu RIGHT-CLICK: [Start] CHOOSE: Open The Start Menu window appears. This folder contains the Programs folder and the shortcut icons that you've placed on the Start menu. To move the Hardware Overview shortcut to the Programs menu, you could simply drag the icon over the Programs folder and drop it in.

Depending on whether you have Administrator rights, you may see a different pop-up menu when you right-click [⏿Start]. For example, an Administrator can install and edit the common applications, in addition to user-specific programs, for everyone to access. Therefore, the Administrator has additional menu options for customizing the Start menu, as illustrated by these graphics.

Default User Group   *Administrator Group*

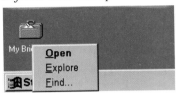 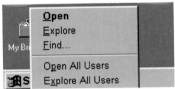

8. To rename the icon and menu command:
   RIGHT-CLICK: Hardware Overview
   CHOOSE: Rename
   TYPE: `Computer Document`
   PRESS: (ENTER)

9. To close the Start Menu window:
   CLICK: its Close button (☒)

10. To display the Start menu:
    CLICK: [⏿Start]

11. To test the new menu command:
    CHOOSE: Computer Document
    WordPad or Microsoft Word will load first and then the document will be opened.

12. To close the word processing application:
    CLICK: Close button (☒) in the application's Title bar

QUICK REFERENCE
Adding a Shortcut to the Start Menu Using Drag and Drop

1. **Open the window containing the file that you want to add to the Start menu.**
2. **DRAG: the file's icon to [⏿Start]**
3. **Release the mouse button to complete the operation.**
4. **Open the Start Menu window if you want to rename the shortcut on the Start menu.**

IN ADDITION INSTALLING APPLICATION SOFTWARE

If you are logged on as an Administrator, the software that you install to your computer is made available to everyone by default. It is referred to as *common* software.

If, on the other hand, you are logged on with User privileges, the software that you install will only be available to your user profile. Other users will not see the program items in their Start menus.

DELETING A SHORTCUT FROM THE START MENU

After adding documents to the Start menu over a period of time, you may decide to remove a shortcut from the Start menu that you no longer use frequently. Removing a shortcut from the menu does not affect the original file. In this section, you practice deleting a shortcut.

Perform the following steps . . .

1. RIGHT-CLICK: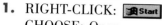
   CHOOSE: Open
   The Start Menu window appears. (*Note*: You may have additional icons displayed in your Start window.)

2. To delete the shortcut:
   RIGHT-CLICK: Computer Document icon
   CHOOSE: Delete
   CLICK: Yes command button to confirm the deletion, if asked

3. Close the Start Menu window.

4. If you click the Start menu, you will notice that the Computer Document shortcut no longer appears. Remember to click on the desktop to remove the Start menu.

QUICK REFERENCE
Deleting a Shortcut

1. **RIGHT-CLICK:** **Start** **to display a shortcut menu**
2. **CHOOSE: Open to display the Start Menu window**
3. **RIGHT-CLICK:** *the shortcut icon* **you want to delete**
4. **CHOOSE: Delete**
5. **CLICK: Yes command button to confirm, if asked**

ADDING A PROGRAM SHORTCUT TO THE START MENU

In addition to adding document files to the Start menu, you can add programs or applications that you use frequently. For example, perhaps you use Windows Word-Pad throughout the day. If you add it to the Start menu, you can access the program directly after clicking the Start button rather than choosing Start, Programs, Accessories, WordPad. In this section, you practice adding an application to the Start menu using the Taskbar Properties dialog box.

Perform the following steps . . .

1. Close all of the open windows on your desktop.

2. You are now going to access the Taskbar Properties dialog box:
   START: Settings, Taskbar
   CLICK: *Start Menu Programs* tab

3. To add a program shortcut to the menu:
   CLICK: Add command button

4. In the Create Shortcut dialog box, specify the name and location of the program file you want to add. In this case, let's add the WordPad accessory to the Start menu:
CLICK: Browse command button
CLICK: down arrow adjacent to the *Look in* drop-down list box
SELECT: ▭ *the drive that contains the Windows NT files*

(*Hint:* You'll know that you're listing the correct drive if you see one or more of the following folders in a window: My Documents, Program Files, and Winnt. In most cases, the Windows NT files are located on drive C:.)

5. Let's find the WordPad executable program file:
DOUBLE-CLICK: Program Files folder icon
DOUBLE-CLICK: Windows NT folder icon
DOUBLE-CLICK: Accessories folder icon
You should see the WordPad accessory name and icon in the Accessories window.

6. To create a shortcut to the WordPad accessory:
DOUBLE-CLICK: WordPad icon
The Create Shortcut dialog box reappears. The path to the shortcut program is shown on the Command line, as shown in Figure 4.3.

FIGURE 4.3

SELECTING THE
PROGRAM FILE

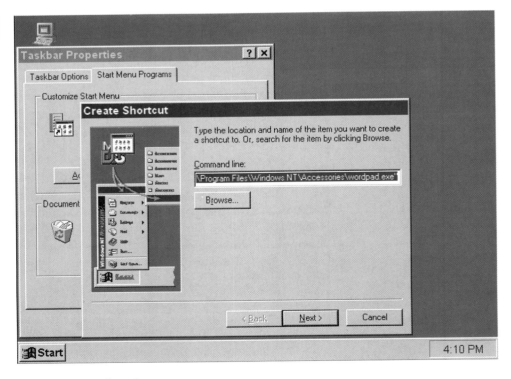

7. To proceed to the next screen:
CLICK: Next >

8. The Select Program Folder dialog box is displayed. If you leave Programs selected, the shortcut will display in the Programs cascading menu. To display the shortcut in the Start menu:
CLICK: Start Menu folder icon
CLICK: Next >

9. Windows now wants to know what to name the shortcut menu option. Let's adjust the name slightly. To complete the procedure:
TYPE: MS Word Pad
CLICK: Finish
CLICK: OK in the Taskbar Properties dialog box

10. To display the Start menu:
CLICK: Start

11. To use the new WordPad menu command:
CHOOSE: MS Word Pad
After a few moments, the initial WordPad screen should display.

12. To close WordPad:
CLICK: its Close button (✕)

Before continuing, let's delete the WordPad shortcut from the Start menu. The procedure is identical to the one you used to delete the document file shortcut.

Perform the following steps . . .

1. RIGHT-CLICK: Start
CHOOSE: Open

2. RIGHT-CLICK: MS Word Pad icon
CHOOSE: Delete
CLICK: Yes command button, if asked

3. Close the Start Menu window.

4. If you display the Start menu, you will notice that the MS Word Pad option no longer appears.

QUICK REFERENCE
Adding a Shortcut to the Start Menu Using the Taskbar Properties Dialog Box

1. START: Settings, Taskbar

2. CLICK: *Start Menu Programs* tab

3. CLICK: Add command button

4. Enter the name of the document, data, or program file you want to display in the Start menu and then click Next >.

5. Select the location where you want the menu item to appear and then click Next >.

6. TYPE: a *name* for the shortcut and then click Finish.

USING THE CONTROL PANEL

With the Control Panel, you can change the system defaults, or properties, of just about any aspect of your computer. For example, you can customize the way your mouse and keyboard work, choose a printer, and customize the appearance of the desktop using color schemes, background patterns, and screen savers. In this section, we describe how you can customize Windows to match your needs and preferences. In the Appendix, you learn more about configuring the network and communications options.

To access the Control Panel window, choose Settings, Control Panel from the Start menu or double-click the Control Panel icon in the "My Computer" window. The Control Panel window contains icons that you select depending on which properties you want to view or edit. Most of the default Control Panel icons are described in Table 4.1.

TABLE 4.1	*Name*	*Icon*	*Configuration Task*
Control Panel Icons	Accessibility Options		Customizes the keyboard, mouse, display, and sound for a person with disabilities
	Add/Remove Programs		Lets you install and uninstall application software and customize your Windows NT Setup
	Console		Sets display options for character-based programs and command prompt windows
	Date/Time		Sets the current date and time, and lets you specify the time zone
	Devices		Lets you start and stop devices and configure options for startup and hardware profiles
	Dial-Up Monitor		Provides a statistical summary for the current dial-up networking connection or modem communications session
	Display		Specifies a desktop background, system colors and fonts, a screen saver, and the screen resolution
	Fonts		Lets you install, remove, and view the fonts available on your computer
	Internet		Customizes the Internet Explorer, including its appearance, proxy servers, start page, mail and news programs, and security options
	Keyboard		Specifies the character repeat rate, cursor blink rate, and keyboard language
	Mail and Fax		Customizes Microsoft Windows Messaging, including Exchange Server and mail services

Table 4.1
Continued

Name	Icon	Configuration Task
Microsoft Mail Postoffice		Lets you administer an existing workgroup postoffice or establish a new postoffice
Modems		Installs or uninstalls a modem; modifies a modem's dialing properties
Mouse		Swaps mouse buttons, specifies double-clicking and tracking speed, and changes pointer shapes
Multimedia		Sets multimedia options and hardware devices, including audio, video, MIDI, and CD music
Network		Specifies your computer name and workgroup, and lets you configure network components, including services, protocols, and adapters
Ports		Specifies communications settings for your serial COM ports, such as baud rate and flow control
Printers		Installs or removes a printer, specifies print spooling options, and modifies properties
Regional Settings		Configures the number, currency, date and time formats for your region of the world
Server		Lets you view and manage the server properties of your computer, including a connection summary and resource usage report
Services		Lets you start and stop services and configure options for startup and hardware profiles
Sounds		Lets you assign sound bites to specific Windows events, such as exiting Windows
System		Provides system information, selects a hardware and user profile, and modifies Windows performance settings
Tape Devices		Specifies properties and device drivers for installed tape backup devices
Telephony		Specifies basic dialing properties and telephony (TAPI) drivers
UPS		Configures the Uninterruptible Power Supply (UPS), if one is connected

In the next few sections, you learn how to customize the desktop display, set the date and time, modify mouse characteristics, change regional settings, and customize the event sounds played by Windows. For more information on the networking utilities, refer to the Appendix.

CUSTOMIZING THE DISPLAY

In this section, you learn to customize the look of the Windows desktop. By default, the Windows desktop displays a teal-colored background and each window displays a dark blue Title bar and gray borders. You can change any of these settings using the Display Properties dialog box. You view the dialog box by double-clicking the Display icon in the Control Panel or by right-clicking on the desktop and then choosing Properties.

Choosing a Background

You can customize the appearance of the desktop's background using patterns or **bitmap graphics** (images stored on disk). To customize the background, double-click the Display icon in the Control Panel. On the *Background* tab of the Display Properties dialog box (Figure 4.4), you select the name of the desired pattern or specify the file containing the bitmap graphic for wallpapering the desktop. You are not limited to the bitmap graphics provided by Windows for your wallpaper. In fact, many organizations use a bitmap graphic of their company logo for wallpaper. After you make a selection, you can view the results without leaving the dialog box by clicking the Apply command button.

In this exercise, you practice manipulating the display of your Windows NT desktop.

Perform the following steps . . .

1. Close any open windows that may appear on the desktop.

2. START: Settings, Control Panel
   The Control Panel window opens onto the desktop.

3. To select a bitmap graphic for wallpapering the desktop:
   DOUBLE-CLICK: Display icon (🖥️)

4. To display the wallpaper bitmap graphic options:
   CLICK: *Background* tab
   SELECT: (None) in the *Pattern* list box
   (*Hint*: The (None) option for both the Pattern and Wallpaper areas appears at the top of the list box.)

5. To fill the desktop with a graphic of blue water in a swimming pool:
   SELECT: Swimming Pool in the *Wallpaper* list box
   (*Note*: Depending on the installation options selected, some wallpaper options may not be available on your system.)

6. To preview the Swimming Pool option:
   CLICK: *Tile* display option below the *Wallpaper* list box
   CLICK: Apply command button
   RIGHT-CLICK: Control Panel button on the taskbar
   CHOOSE: Minimize
   You should now be able to see the background wallpaper.

7. Let's select another wallpaper option:
SELECT: Coffee Bean in the *Wallpaper* list box
CLICK: *Center* display option and watch the preview monitor
CLICK: *Tile* display option and watch the preview monitor
CLICK: Apply command button
The Tile option reproduces the bitmap graphic until it fills the entire desktop. The Center option places only one copy of the bitmap graphic at the center of the screen. Your screen should now appear similar to Figure 4.4.

FIGURE 4.4

SELECTING A
BACKGROUND IN
THE DISPLAY PROPERTIES
DIALOG BOX

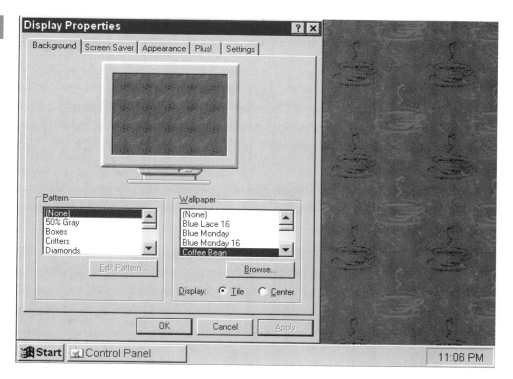

8. On your own, practice applying other options from the *Wallpaper* list box.

9. To apply a pattern to the desktop:
SELECT: (None) in the *Wallpaper* list box to remove your previous selections
SELECT: Thatches in the *Pattern* list box
CLICK: Apply command button
The desktop's background is covered in a thatch-like pattern.

10. On your own, practice applying other options from the Pattern area.

11. Before proceeding, do the following:
SELECT: (None) in the *Wallpaper* list box
SELECT: (None) in the *Pattern* list box
CLICK: OK to accept these choices as final

12. Close the Control Panel window by right-clicking its button on the taskbar and then choosing the Close command.

1. **START: Settings, Control Panel**
2. **DOUBLE-CLICK: Display icon (🖥️)**
3. **SELECT:** *Background tab*
4. **SELECT: a Pattern or Wallpaper option**
5. **CLICK: Apply command button to preview your selections**
6. **CLICK: OK command button**

Using a Screen Saver

Screen savers were created to protect the image quality of your monitor. When a static, unchanging image is displayed on the monitor for extended periods of time, the image tends to become etched into the monitor. A screen saver program automatically blanks your screen, or displays random moving objects, to avoid burning in a screen image when a monitor is left on for prolonged periods of time. With today's monitors, the problem of "burning" isn't as prevalent. However, screen savers are fun to look at and are being used today for security reasons. Windows screen savers incorporate password protection, which requires you to enter a password before removing the screen saver utility and returning to your work.

To select and customize a screen saver, you open the Display Properties dialog box and then click on the *Screen Saver* tab.

1. **RIGHT-CLICK:** *an empty part of the desktop*
2. **CHOOSE: Properties**
3. **CLICK:** *Screen Saver tab*
4. **SELECT: an option from the** *Screen Saver* **drop-down list box**
5. **CLICK: OK command button**

Changing Color Schemes

Whether you use a 17-inch color, 12-inch monochrome monitor, or a liquid crystal display (LCD screens are common in laptop and notebook computers), you will appreciate the variety of color schemes available for Windows.

In this exercise, you change the Windows color scheme.

 **Perform the following steps . . .**

1. To open the Display Properties dialog box using a shortcut:
    RIGHT-CLICK: *an empty part of the desktop*
    CHOOSE: Properties

2. To modify the screen colors:
    CLICK: *Appearance* tab

3. Let's review the available options:
    CLICK: down arrow for the *Scheme* drop-down list box
    Your screen should appear similar, but not identical, to Figure 4.5.

FIGURE 4.5

DISPLAY PROPERTIES
DIALOG BOX:
APPEARANCE TAB

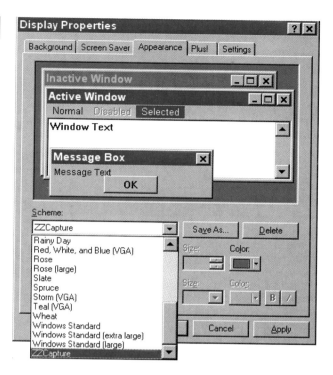

4. To sample various color schemes:
   PRESS: ⬆ and ⬇ multiple times to scroll through the list
   Notice that the sample preview window above the drop-down list box displays the highlighted color scheme.

5. SELECT: *your favorite color scheme*
   CLICK: Apply command button

6. Before proceeding, do the following:
   SELECT: Windows Standard from the *Scheme* drop-down list box
   CLICK: OK command button

QUICK REFERENCE
Changing Color Schemes

1. **RIGHT-CLICK:** *an empty part of the desktop*
2. **CHOOSE:** Properties
3. **CLICK:** *Appearance* tab
4. **SELECT:** a color scheme from the *Scheme* drop-down list box
5. **CLICK:** Apply command button to preview your selection
6. **CLICK:** OK command button

SETTING THE DATE/TIME

If you often use a laptop computer and are "on the move" in different time zones, you may need to change the date and time on your computer. Although you can set the date/time from the Control Panel, the easiest method is by double-clicking the clock on the taskbar. In this section, you practice making date and time adjustments.

Perform the following steps . . .

1. DOUBLE-CLICK: the clock on the taskbar
   The Date/Time Properties dialog box appears.

2. If necessary, make changes in the dialog box to reflect your current date and time. To change the month or year, use the *Month* drop-down list box and the *Year* spin box. To change the day, click the correct date in the calendar area. To change the time, click in the digital time clock area and edit the time by typing or by clicking the spin box.

3. To close the Date/Time Properties dialog box:
   CLICK: OK command button

QUICK REFERENCE
Customizing the
Date/Time

1. **DOUBLE-CLICK: the clock on the taskbar**

2. **Edit the date and time.**

3. **CLICK: OK command button**

MODIFYING MOUSE CHARACTERISTICS

Are you left-handed? Well, Microsoft has not forgotten about our left-handed friends in this world. To prove that they take left-handers seriously, just look to the Mouse Pointers dialog box. You access this dialog box by double-clicking the Mouse icon ( ) in the Control Panel window. On the *Buttons* tab of the Mouse Pointers dialog box, you can switch from a right-handed mouse orientation to a left-handed orientation. You can also speed up or slow down the double-clicking speed. For novice users, a slower double-clicking speed is easier to learn and use.

Let's demonstrate how to modify your mouse's behavior.

Perform the following steps . . .

1. START: Settings, Control Panel
   The Control Panel window opens onto the desktop.

2. To modify the mouse characteristics:
   DOUBLE-CLICK: Mouse icon ( )

3. CLICK: *Buttons* tab

4. To adjust the speed required to register a double-click:
   DRAG: slider bar in the *Double-click speed* area all the way to the left

5. In the *Test area*:
   DOUBLE-CLICK: the jack-in-the-box with a pause between the first and second click
   If a double-click is recognized, Jack shows himself. You can try double-clicking again to send Jack back into the box.

6. If necessary, speed up the double-click until you get the Jack in the jack-in-the-box to appear and disappear consistently.

7. DRAG: slider bar to the right (to about 75% of top speed)

8. DOUBLE-CLICK: the jack-in-the-box
   Notice that you must double-click the figure faster to elicit the same response.

9. Move the slider bar to the speed level you are most comfortable with.

10. To close the Mouse Properties dialog box:
    CLICK: OK command button

QUICK REFERENCE
Modifying Mouse
Characteristics

1. **START: Settings, Control Panel**
2. **DOUBLE-CLICK: Mouse icon (****)**
3. **CLICK: *Buttons* tab**
4. **SELECT: a double-clicking speed**
5. **SELECT: a right- or left-handed orientation**
6. **CLICK: OK command button**

CHANGING REGIONAL SETTINGS

Windows provides over 50 regional settings from which you can choose how to display numbers, currency amounts, and the date and time. These settings differ depending on the country you're in. Outside the United States, for example, the date is often displayed as DD/MM/YY. In Europe, amounts are often displayed with the decimal and comma swapped, as in the following example: 4.300,00. To adjust these settings, you make selections from the Regional Settings Properties dialog box.

Perform the following steps . . .

1. Ensure that the Control Panel window appears open on the desktop.

2. To see the regional settings that are in effect on your computer:
   DOUBLE-CLICK: Regional Settings icon (●)

3. To see the assumptions Windows makes about numbers:
   CLICK: *Number* tab
   The dialog box in Figure 4.6 shows how Windows displays numbers in the United States.

FIGURE 4.6

IN THE UNITED STATES, WINDOWS DISPLAYS NUMBERS ACCORDING TO THESE ASSUMPTIONS

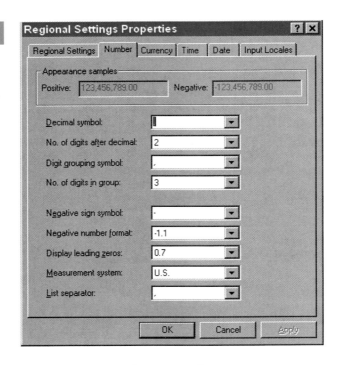

4. To view the other regional settings:
   CLICK: the *Currency*, *Time*, and *Date* tabs

5. To close the Regional Settings Properties dialog box:
   CLICK: OK command button

QUICK REFERENCE
Changing Regional Settings

1. **START: Settings, Control Center**
2. **DOUBLE-CLICK: Regional Settings icon ( )**
3. **CLICK: *Regional Settings* tab**
4. **SELECT: your country from the drop-down list box**
5. **Make additional changes to the regional settings, as required.**
6. **CLICK: OK command button**

CONTROLLING SOUND EVENTS

If you have a sound card installed in your computer, you will hear different sounds depending on the current "event." A Windows event is a general term that refers to a Windows action such as exiting Windows or maximizing a window. By default, Windows applies specific sounds to limited events. You can change or add to these sounds by displaying the Sounds Properties dialog box from the Control Panel window. Let's demonstrate this fun and functional utility.

Perform the following steps . . .

1. Ensure that the Control Panel window appears open on the desktop.

2. DOUBLE-CLICK: Sounds icon (🔊)
   The Sounds Properties dialog box appears. The events in the list box that have a loudspeaker next to the icon play a sound when activated.

3. To scroll through the list of Windows events:
   CLICK: down arrow on the scroll bar repeatedly in the *Events* list box

4. To hear the sound associated with exiting windows:
   SELECT: Exit Windows
   CLICK: Play button (▶) next to the Preview area
   (*Note*: You must have a sound card properly configured in your computer in order to play sounds.)

5. To see the other sounds that you can choose from:
   CLICK: down arrow adjacent to the *Name* drop-down list box

6. Scroll through the drop-down list box to see the sounds that you can associate to an event.

7. Let's leave the sound settings unchanged. Before continuing, close all windows that are open on the desktop.

QUICK REFERENCE
Controlling Sound Events

1. START: Settings, Control Center
2. DOUBLE-CLICK: Sound icon (🔊)
3. SELECT: an event or action from the *Events* list box
4. SELECT: a sound from the *Name* drop-down list box
5. CLICK: OK command button

USING THE PRINTERS FOLDER

The Printers folder provides a centralized location for installing or uninstalling a printer, changing printer settings, and checking or changing the status of scheduled print jobs. You access the Printers folder by choosing Settings, Printers from the Start menu. You can also double-click the Printers folder in the "My Computer" window.

In a multitasking environment, application programs must share processing time, memory, and printer resources. When you send several documents to the same printer one after the other, Windows NT coordinates the printing by placing the documents temporarily in a print spooler or queue on the hard disk. When the printer has completed one print job, Windows takes the next print job from the queue and feeds it to the printer. Because this spooling process occurs in the background, you can continue working in an application immediately after you send a document to the printer.

The Windows NT print spooler is a full 32-bit application, which means you realize little or no slow-down when you send a document to the printer and return to your application. To monitor the documents in the print spooler, you simple double-click the printer name in the Printers folder. You can manipulate the print queue by reordering and deleting files that appear in the list. For example, if you want to print a one-page letter after sending several larger documents to the printer, you can move the letter up in the print queue so that it is the next document in line for the printer. To move a file in the queue, you simply drag the filename using the mouse and drop it further up in the queue.

By choosing the Printer, Document Defaults command from the queue window, you can also change the default printer settings. Figure 4.7 shows the dialog box that appears when the *Advanced* tab is selected. As you select options in the top window, such as Paper Size, Orientation, and Resolution, the bottom window changes to display the options that are available. This dialog box provides you with tremendous power and control for configuring your printer.

FIGURE 4.7

PRINTER DIALOG BOX

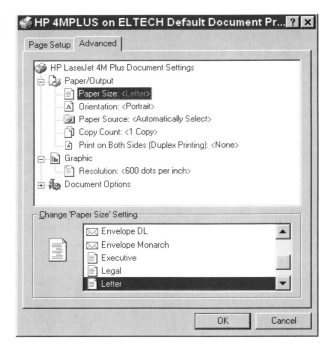

CHOOSING A PRINTER

To add a new printer to your computer system, double-click the Add Printer icon in the Printers folder. This action launches the Add Printer Wizard which leads you through installing the printer driver for your printer. A **printer driver** is software that enables an application program to communicate with your printer.

To change the property settings of an installed printer, you point to the printer name in the Printers folder and right-click with the mouse. When you choose the Properties command, the dialog box in Figure 4.8 appears allowing you to specify security options, scheduling priorities, and device settings (the current tab displayed in Figure 4.8.)

FIGURE 4.8

PRINTER PROPERTIES
DIALOG BOX: DEVICE
SETTINGS TAB

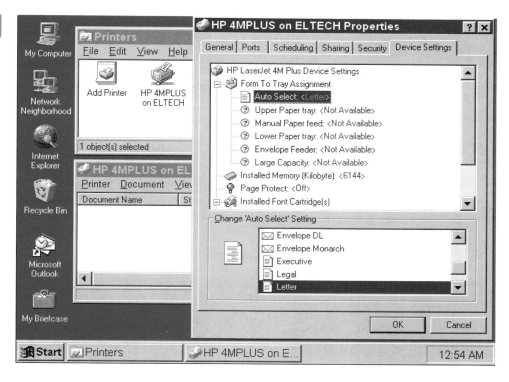

If you require further assistance with printing, refer to the online Help facility and search for "Printers."

Summary

This session explored different ways of customizing Windows. First, you added a file shortcut and a program shortcut to the Start menu. From the Control Panel window, you examined the Display option for customizing the "look" of the Windows desktop and the Date/Time, Mouse, Regional Settings, and Sound options. You were also introduced to the process of installing and uninstalling software programs. The session concluded with a description of the Printers folder including how to change the status of scheduled print jobs and how to modify a printer's properties.

COMMAND SUMMARY

Many of the commands and procedures appearing in this session are provided in the command summary in Table 4.2.

TABLE 4.2	*Task Description*	*General Instruction*
Command Summary	Add a shortcut to the Start menu	Right-drag a program or document icon to the Start button.
	Delete a shortcut from the Start menu	Right-click the Start button and choose the Open command. Drag the shortcut you want to delete to the Recycle Bin.
	Choose a background for the desktop	Right-click on the desktop and choose the Properties command. Click the *Background* tab and then select a pattern or wallpaper option. Click OK to continue.
	Use a screen saver	Right-click on the desktop and choose the Properties command. Click the *Screen Saver* tab and then select a screen saver option. Click OK to continue.
	Change color schemes	Right-click on the desktop and choose the Properties command. Click the *Appearance* tab and then select a color scheme. Click OK to continue.
	Customize the Date/Time	Double-click the clock on the taskbar to display the Date/Time dialog box.
	Change regional settings	Choose Settings, Control Panel from the Start menu. Double-click the Regional Settings icon.
	Control sound events	Choose Settings, Control Panel from the Start menu. Double-click the Sound icon.
	Modify a printer's properties	Choose Settings, Printers from the Start menu. Right-click the desired printer and choose Properties.

KEY TERMS

bitmap graphics

A graphic image or picture that is stored in a disk file as a series or pattern of dots.

group

A collection of user accounts; a method of organizing rights and permissions and then applying them to a number of users. Windows NT provides several built-in groups.

permissions

For a shared resource, such as a file, directory, or disk drive, the rights a user has to access and manipulate the resource.

printer driver

A file containing instructions that enable a software program to communicate with a printer.

user profile

Configuration information that is saved for a particular person. If stored on a server, a user profile can be accessed by the user from any other computer that is connected to the server. If stored on a local computer, a user profile is primarily a logon specification for a customized environment.

EXERCISES

SHORT ANSWER

1. How do you change the color scheme of the Windows desktop?

2. What is meant by the phrase *wallpaper your desktop*?

3. What are some benefits of using a screen saver?

4. How do you add a document or program to the Start menu?

5. How do you rename a shortcut that you've added to the Start menu?

6. How do you delete a shortcut that you've added to the Start menu?

7. In Windows, what does your selection of a "regional setting" affect?

8. Name two settings available for the Starfield Simulation screen saver.

9. What Control Panel utility would you use to view a statistical summary of a modem communications session?

10. What Control Panel utility would you use to view the network users who are connected to and accessing your computer's shared resources?

HANDS-ON

(*Note*: Ensure that you know the storage location of your Advantage Files and your Data Files before proceeding.)

1. In this exercise, you use the Paint accessory program to create a new wallpaper bitmap for your desktop.

    a. START: Programs, Accessories, Paint

    b. CLICK: Brush icon (🖌)

    c. To draw with a wide brush stroke:
       CLICK: the first option in the second row of the pattern area (■)

    d. To draw using a specific color:
       CLICK: *any color* with the left mouse button

    e. Drag the mouse on the desktop to write "*your name's* Computer!" similar to the text in Figure 4.9. Try to write the text in the bottom-right area of the Paint window so that the wallpaper will appear more centered on the desktop. (*Note:* If you aren't pleased with your drawing, choose Edit, Undo from the Menu bar and try again.)

    f. Let's save this image to your Data Files location:
       CHOOSE: File, Save As
       CLICK: down arrow beside the *Save in* drop-down list box
       SELECT: *your Data Files location*

    g. To type a name for the file:
       DOUBLE-CLICK: "untitled" text in the *File name* text box
       TYPE: `MyWallPaper`

    h. To select a format for the file:
       CLICK: down arrow beside the *Save as type* drop-down list box
       SELECT: 16 Color Bitmap

    i. CLICK: Save command button

    j. To display the Paint image as wallpaper:
       CHOOSE: File, Set As Wallpaper (Tiled)

    k. Exit Paint.

    l. The Paint image should now appear on your desktop (Figure 4.9).

    m. Let's assume that you must share your computer with someone else in the office. To remove this image from the desktop:
       START: Settings, Control Panel
       DOUBLE-CLICK: Display icon (🖥)
       CLICK: *Background* tab
       Notice that your Paint file, MyWallPaper, appears in the list box.

    n. To remove the wallpaper:
       SELECT: (None) in the *Wallpaper* list box
       CLICK: OK command button

    o. Close any open windows that appear on your desktop.

FIGURE 4.9

USING A PAINT IMAGE
AS WALLPAPER ON
THE DESKTOP

2. In this exercise, you change the color scheme of the desktop.

    a. Using the shortcut method, open the Display Properties dialog box.

    b. Click the *Appearance* tab.

    c. Select a color scheme.

    d. Display the color scheme in the desktop.

    e. Change the color scheme back to its former selection.

3. This exercise lets you practice choosing a screen saver.

    a. Using the shortcut method, open the Display Properties dialog box.

    b. Click the *Screen Saver* tab.

    c. Select a screen saver.

    d. Specify the settings for the selected screen saver.

    e. Preview the screen saver on the desktop.

    f. Direct Windows to display the screen saver after five minutes of inactivity.

    g. Change the screen saver setting back to "None."

4. In this exercise, you practice adding the Calculator program to the Start menu using the Taskbar Properties dialog box. Do the following:

   a. START: Settings, Taskbar

   b. SELECT: *Start Menu Programs* tab

   c. CLICK: Add option

   d. Browse the hard disk to locate the Calculator program. The calculator program is named "Calc." (*Hint:* Search in the SYSTEM32 folder located in the WINNT folder on drive C:.)

   e. DOUBLE-CLICK: Calc program icon

   f. CLICK: Next >

   g. To store the shortcut in the Start menu:
      CLICK: Start Menu icon
      CLICK: Next >

   h. Enter a new menu name for the program shortcut:
      TYPE: `Calculator`

   i. CLICK: Finish

   j. Close the Taskbar Properties window by clicking the OK command button and then display the Start menu. The Calculator option should appear at the top of the menu.

   k. Practice launching the Calculator program.

   l. On your own, delete the Calculator program from the Start menu.

5. **On Your Own:** Previewing the Utilities in Control Panel
   In this exercise, you simply open the Control Panel window and then double-click each icon to preview its dialog box. If there is a Help command button in the dialog box, click the button to peruse the Help Topics for the utility. If there are tabs in the dialog box, make sure that you click each one to see the set of options available. This exploratory method of previewing the Control Panel utilities is an excellent way to learn about your system. Finally, make some notes on which utilities appear in your Control Panel window and which ones provide help.

6. **On Your Own:** Changing the Appearance of Your Desktop
   In this exercise, you open the Display Properties dialog box and then click on each tab to change your desktop's appearance. First, select your favorite wallpaper option. Then, choose a screen saver and specify its settings. Then, select your favorite color scheme. Finally, peruse the other tabs available in the Display Properties dialog box.

THE RIVER REPORT

(*Note*: In the following case problems, assume the role of the primary characters and perform the same steps that they identify. You may want to re-read the session opening.)

1. It's 6:30 PM and Linda James is seeing red—actually, neon pink, lime green, and purple. The existing colors of her Windows desktop have given Linda an amazing headache and her stomach is urging her to retire for dinner. Realizing now that customizing the desktop is relatively simple, she decides to apply a standard color scheme, wallpaper, and screen saver, and then call it a night. After a few moments of scanning the options, she settles on the "Desert" color scheme, "Solstice" wallpaper, and the "3D Flying Objects (OpenGL)" screen saver with a 10-minute delay. In only a few minutes, she completely revises the look of her desktop. Lastly, she opens the Control Panel window and resizes it to appear similar to Figure 4.10. With her work behind her now, she leaves the office by 6:45 PM.

FIGURE 4.10

LINDA'S DESKTOP WITH
A STOCK BACKGROUND

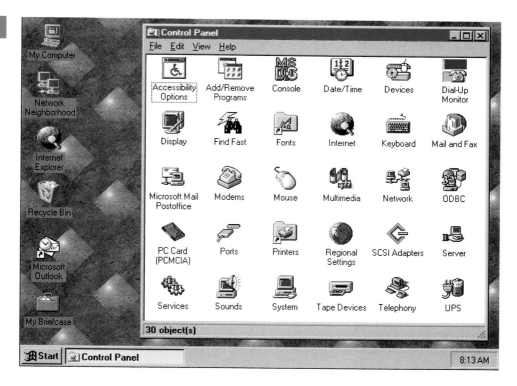

2. Upon opening the door to her office in the morning, Linda is surprised to see Hank working on her computer. "Hi Linda! I just need to remove some of my personal files and paintings. I hope you don't mind." Linda assured him that she didn't mind, but in truth, she minded very much. She, too, has some personal files on the machine.

As soon as Hank leaves, Linda closes the Control Panel window and uses Paint to put a message on her desktop. She wants to discourage anyone from using her computer without her permission. (*Hint*: See Hands-On exercise 1 for hints on how to use Paint to create a wallpaper bitmap.) She uses the Text tool to write the message and then saves the file as 16 Color Bitmap called "MorePaper" to her Data Files location. Lastly, she changes her color scheme to Red, White, and Blue (VGA). When finished, her desktop looks like Figure 4.11.

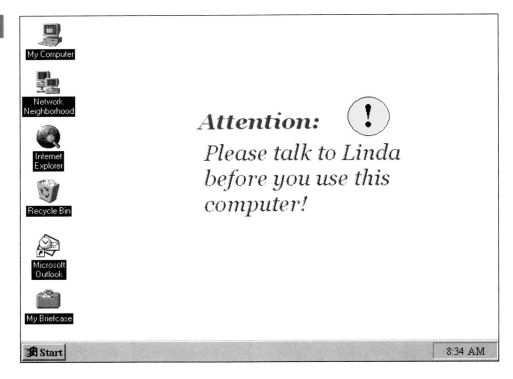

FIGURE 4.11

LINDA'S DESKTOP WITH A CUSTOM BACKGROUND

3. Linda decides to customize the desktop further by adding the Notepad program to the Start menu. Pleased with herself, she then loads Notepad using the new menu option. Satisfied that the option works, she exits Notepad and gets back to work.

4. In reviewing the notes from the last staff meeting held by Hank Leary, Linda's predecessor, Linda notices several agenda items concerning the need for another printer in the front office. Because the reasons for wanting the printer are valid and there is a budget available for hardware purchases, she decides to surprise the staff by buying a new laser printer with all the bells and whistles. Flipping through the yellow pages, Linda spots a local computer dealer and phones their sales line. After holding for more than 10 minutes, Linda gets a salesperson who provides her with the following misinformation:

Well ma'am, you see, you don't really need to use Windows NT to send multiple documents to the printer at the same time. Heck, with our printers, you don't even need to have a printer driver for Windows. Now the real reason that you don't want to print with Windows is that printing uses all of your computer's memory or RAM for something called print spoiling. And with spoiling, you can't continue to work in your programs because all the RAM is used by the spoiler. See what you get when printing in Windows. So, you'd be much better off buying one of Lying Lou's Lazy Laser products. They're just supreme!

Write a summary stating why the above information is incorrect and provide Linda with the honest facts about printing in Windows NT.

5. Linda decides to perform one more small task before calling it a day. She deletes the Notepad option from the Start menu because she will be using WordPad more in the future. She needs to use the formatting commands that are available in WordPad. Also, she resets her desktop to the default Windows schemes, including (None) for the wallpaper and Windows Standard for the color scheme.

Appendix

Microsoft Windows NT 4.0
Advanced Topics

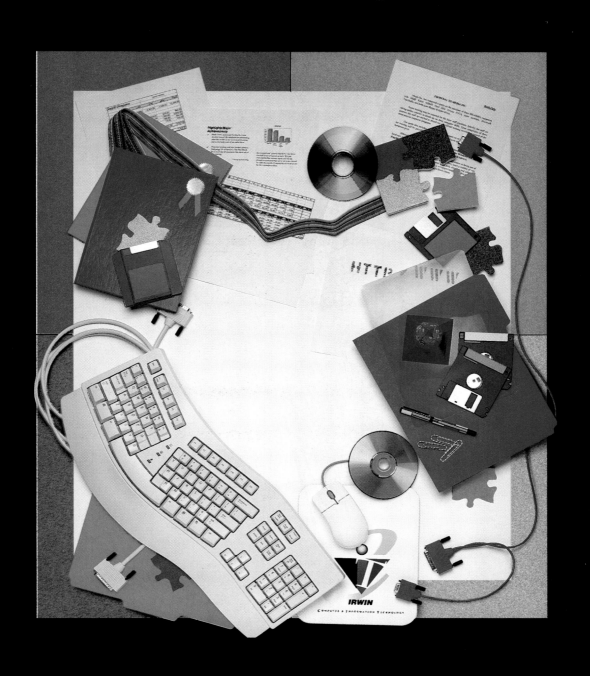

SESSION OUTLINE

INTRODUCTION

Network and modem technologies let you travel beyond the desktop. In addition to some extra hardware requirements, you will need software to implement and administrate your networking and communications tasks. With Windows NT, many of these tools are already built into the operating system. Because we cannot ensure that everybody has a network or modem connection (or Administrator rights), this session is included as an appendix. We concentrate less on the hands-on exercises and more on describing the advanced capabilities of Windows NT.

ADMINISTRATIVE TOOLS

Windows NT Workstation 4.0 provides several administrative tools for managing your disk and network resources. You access these tools using the Start, Administrative Tools (Common) command. While some of these commands require Administrator rights, it is still advantageous for you to know which tools perform these important tasks. The cascading menu that appears in Figure A.1 displays the following utilities: Backup, Disk Administrator, Event Viewer, Performance Monitor, Remote Access Admin, User Manager, and Windows NT Diagnostics.

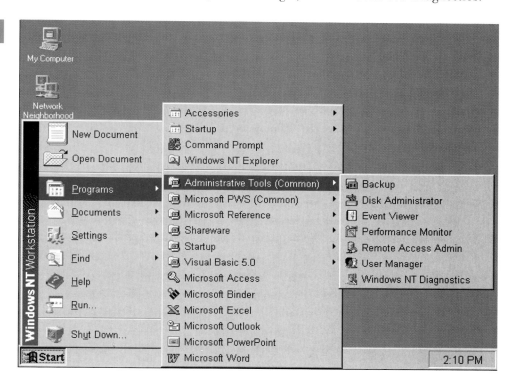

This section describes briefly each of these administrative tools. You can choose to explore them as they are discussed in the guide or do so on your own. If you follow along with the guide, ensure that you close each program prior to launching the next administrative tool.

Backup
If you have a tape drive installed in your computer, the NT Backup command lets you copy your hard disk data to tape. You should protect yourself from the accidental loss or corruption of data by performing a **backup** of your hard disk regularly. Although NT Backup supports only tape drives, you can use other software and media, such as removable disks, CD-Recordable discs, and floppy diskettes, to perform a backup.

Disk Administrator
The Disk Administrator utility lets you (as an Administrator) prepare hard disks for storage using either the NTFS or FAT file systems. Similar to the FDISK command in MS-DOS, you use this utility to create and remove **partitions** and logical

drives. For more information on the available file systems, choose the Help command from the Start menu and then search for "file systems" using the *Index* tab.

Event Viewer
This utility lets you monitor the events that take place in your computer system. An **event** is any occurrence or activity that requires NT to notify the user. Each time that you start NT, the Event Viewer begins storing events in three separate logs:
- *System log*, which records events such as the failure to load a driver
- *Security log*, which tracks changes to the security system
- *Application log*, which logs program-specific information

Performance Monitor
Analyze and monitor the performance of any computer attached to the network in terms of its processor, memory, threads, processes, and more. You can even display data from more than one computer simultaneously. The information is typically presented graphically in a chart or listed in a report.

Remote Access Admin
The Remote Access Administrator utility lets you start and manage the **Remote Access Service (RAS)**. Using this utility, you can specify dial-in permissions for remote users and limit access to the network that may lie beyond the server.

User Manager
You use this utility to specify security policies and determine how other users on a network gain access to your computer. The User Manager lets you create and manage user accounts and groups, along with their rights and permissions. You must have Administrator rights in order to perform these tasks.

Windows NT Diagnostics
A diagnostic tool that allows you to view and print system information, typically for technical support personnel. Let's review briefly the information contained on each of the nine tabs:
- *Version* tab: Windows NT version, build, and serial number
- *System* tab: BIOS and CPU information
- *Display* tab: name, BIOS, and configuration of graphics adapter
- *Drives* tab: storage devices and their properties
- *Memory* tab: physical and kernel memory, and pagefile space
- *Services* tab: state of services and devices
- *Resources* tab: IRQs, port and memory addresses, and DMA channels
- *Environment* tab: environmental variables for system and local user
- *Network* tab: domain and workgroup, transports, settings, and statistics

SETTING UP A MODEM

Before you can communicate over the phone lines, your computer system must have a modem that has been properly installed and is recognized by Windows NT. You only have to install the modem once to use the communications features described in this appendix. In the following section, you learn how to install a new modem.

Perform the following steps . . .

1. Make sure the modem is properly attached to your computer's serial port, if it is an external modem. If you own an internal modem, follow the manufacturer's installation guidelines for removing your computer's case, identifying an appropriate expansion slot, and then plugging in the internal modem card.

2. If you are using an external modem, turn the power on so that Windows NT can communicate with it during the setup procedure. Also, you should connect your modem to the telephone line jack.

3. Start Windows NT and log on to the system.

4. From the Start menu:
CHOOSE: Settings, Control Panel
DOUBLE-CLICK: Modems icon (📞)
The dialog box in Figure A.2 will appear. (*Note*: Figure A.2 shows one modem already configured for this computer system. You would not typically add more than one modem to your computer.)

FIGURE A.2

MODEMS DIALOG BOX

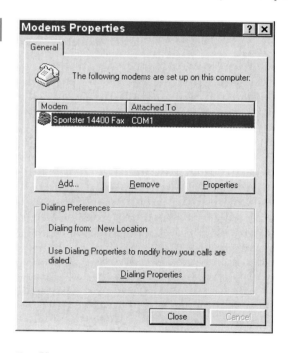

5. You must now load the proper modem drivers. Do the following:
CLICK: Add command button

6. Using the Install New Modem wizard, select the appropriate modem type. Windows NT will load the required drivers, as necessary. To proceed through the wizard, make selections and click the Next command button. (*Note*: You may need to place the original Windows NT installation CD-ROM into the drive, so that any additional drivers may be loaded.)

7. After following the on-screen instructions, click the Finish command button to save your modem settings and return to the Control Panel.

QUICK REFERENCE
Installing a New Modem

1. **Ensure that the modem is properly installed.**
2. **START: Settings, Control Panel**
3. **DOUBLE-CLICK: Modems icon (📞)**
4. **Follow the installation instructions in the Install New Modem wizard.**
5. **CLICK: [Finish] to save the modem settings**

Now that your modem is installed, you can load the Windows modem communications software utilities described in Table A.1. In the Control Panel window, you double-click the Add/Remove Programs icon (⊞) and then select the *Windows NT Setup* tab. With the *Communications* check box highlighted, click the Details button to view and select the optional communications utilities. If you add or remove options in this window, ensure that you have the original Windows NT installation CD-ROM inserted into the drive.

TABLE A.1

Some Communications Utilities

Name	Icon	Function
HyperTerminal		Communicate with another computer or communication service, such as AT&T Mail, MCI Mail, or CompuServe.
Phone Dialer		Manage phone calls from your computer, including dialing and logging your calls.
Microsoft Exchange		Send and receive e-mail across the Internet or using a Microsoft Mail Post Office.

In the following section, we describe the basics of sending and receiving mail with Microsoft Exchange, which was recently renamed to Windows Messaging. You then learn how to institute a dial-up networking session and connect to the World Wide Web using the Microsoft Internet Explorer. Lastly, we describe the Microsoft Peer Web Services.

USING MICROSOFT EXCHANGE

Microsoft Exchange is what you use in Windows NT to manage, create, send, and receive electronic messages called *e-mail*. Exchange is often referred to as the universal inbox because it provides a single place for you to receive your incoming mail. If you have installed Microsoft Office 97, you may see the Microsoft Outlook icon (📧) on your desktop rather than the Inbox icon (📬). While both programs provide access to electronic mail, they differ in their setup and functionality. This section describes the Microsoft Exchange Inbox only. For more information on Outlook, refer to the Microsoft Office 97 Help.

LOADING EXCHANGE

If Microsoft Exchange is already set up on your computer, you load it by double-clicking the Inbox icon (📬) on the desktop. The Microsoft Exchange Viewer will display, similar to the screen showing in Figure A.3. (*Note*: If folders aren't displaying in the left pane of the window on your computer, choose View, Folders from the Menu bar.) The first time you double-click the Inbox icon (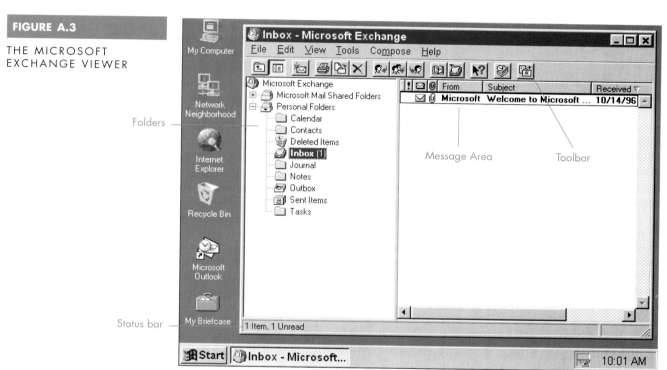) on the desktop, Exchange displays a Setup Wizard that asks you a few questions. Your answers are stored in an Exchange profile which determines such details as where to store your incoming mail.

FIGURE A.3

THE MICROSOFT
EXCHANGE VIEWER

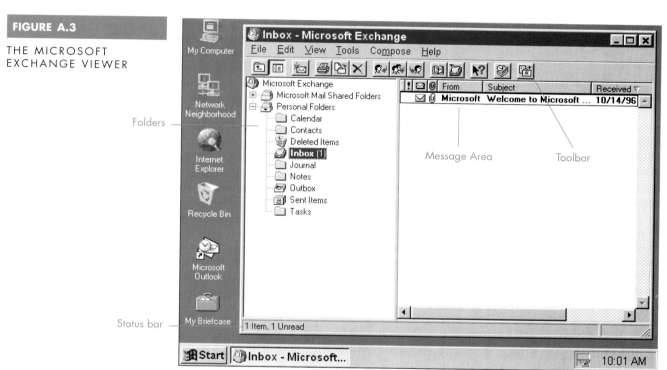

SENDING AND RECEIVING MESSAGES

Microsoft Exchange provides you with tools for creating e-mail messages that you would expect to find only in a full-featured word processing application. Exchange lets you format your messages and supports OLE, which means you can copy objects created in other Windows applications, such as an Excel chart, into your e-mail message. However, you may find that some mail systems only support plain-text documents, and not the rich-text documents of Exchange. These mail systems include CompuServe and most of the POP servers on the Internet. For these services, Exchange sends a stripped-down or plain-text version of your document and attaches embedded objects as separate files.

To compose an e-mail message, you click the New Message button (📧) on the Exchange toolbar. You can also choose Compose, New Message from the Menu bar. In the New Message window, you click the To button to display a list of entries from your Address Book. You select an entry by double-clicking the desired name. To send the message to more than one person, you simply continue selecting names from your Address Book. Exchange automatically separates these names with a semicolon. You can also select names to carbon copy by clicking the Cc button and following the same process. After entering descriptive text in the *Subject* text box, you begin writing the e-mail message.

When the message is complete, you click the Send button (⊠) to send the e-mail message to your Outbox. If you are not connected to a network, the message will remain in your Outbox until you choose the Tools, Deliver Now command from the Menu bar. Exchange will either connect you to the Internet, if you have an Internet account, or to an online service. Once the message is sent, it is removed from your Outbox. At the same time that you send mail, you can also retrieve incoming mail. Your new mail will display in the Inbox folder in bold type. To read your e-mail, you simply double-click the message.

QUICK REFERENCE
Compose a New Message

1. **CLICK: New Message button (⊠) on the Exchange toolbar**
2. **SELECT: *the recipient* using the To button**
3. **Enter the subject and body text for the e-mail message.**
4. **CLICK: Send button (⊠) to send the message to your Outbox**

QUICK REFERENCE
Sending and Receiving Messages

1. **CHOOSE: Tools, Deliver Now from the Menu bar**
2. **SELECT: *Send Mail* check box**
3. **SELECT: *Retrieve Mail* check box**
4. **CLICK: OK command button**

IN ADDITION REPLYING TO A MESSAGE

1. To reply to a message:

   — CLICK: Reply to Sender button (⊠)

   — CLICK: Reply to All button (⊠)

— CLICK: Forward button (⊠)

2. Complete your reply as you would write a new message.

3. CLICK: Send button (⊠)

DIAL-UP NETWORKING

The Dial-Up Networking utility lets you, as a remote user, connect to a Windows NT Server that is running the Remote Access Service (RAS). For example, you can use dial-up networking with a modem to connect to your office computer from your home, access an important document stored on your office network, modify the document, and then print it on your office laser printer so that it is waiting for you in the morning. You can also use dial-up networking to connect to the World Wide Web through an Internet Service Provider (ISP). In this section, you learn how to set up an access account using the NT Dial-Up Networking utility.

You begin a dial-up session by double-clicking the Dial-Up Networking utility in the "My Computers" window. To establish a connection from the resulting dialog box, you select an entry from the *Phonebook* drop-down list box and then click the Dial command button. Once connected, you typically enter a username, password, and the network server's domain name to which you want access. Then, you can minimize the utility and proceed as if you were connected locally to the network.

In this section, you learn how to add a phonebook entry for dial-up networking.

Perform the following steps . . .

1. Ensure that Windows NT is started and that you are logged on.

2. To display the Dial-Up Networking dialog box:
   DOUBLE-CLICK: "My Computer" icon (🖥️)

   DOUBLE-CLICK: Dial-Up Networking icon (📇)
   Alternatively, you can choose the Programs, Accessories, Dial-Up Networking command from the Start menu.

3. In the New Phonebook Entry Wizard dialog box:
   TYPE: My New Connection
   CLICK: Next command button
   (*Hint*: Do not select the check box that appears on this page.)

4. In the Server dialog box, you specify who you are connecting to. Let's assume that you want to call your local Internet Service Provider:
   SELECT: *I am calling the Internet* check box
   CLICK: Next command button

5. In the Phone Number dialog box, you will enter a fictitious entry:
   SELECT: United States of America (1) in the *Country Code* drop-down list box
   TYPE: *your area code* in the *Area code* drop-down list box
   TYPE: 555-1234 in the *Phone Number* text box

6. To complete the addition:
   CLICK: Next command button
   CLICK: Finish command button
   You are returned to the original dialog box and your new entry is selected in the *Phonebook* drop-down list box.

7. Let's view some of the customizing options for this new entry:
   CLICK: More command button once
   Your screen should now appear similar to Figure A.4.

FIGURE A.4

DIAL-UP NETWORKING
WINDOW

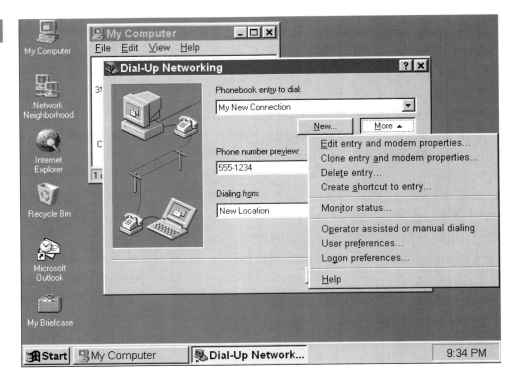

8. CHOOSE: Edit entry and modem properties command
   A dialog box appears with the following tabs: *Basic, Server, Script, Security,* and *X.25.* On the *Basic* tab, you can edit the information that you entered in the last seven steps. On the *Server* tab, you specify the server type and network protocols used at the other end of the connection. The remaining tabs are used for setting up advanced configurations.

9. To remove the dialog box:
   CLICK: Cancel command button

10. To access another useful feature in dial-up networking:
    CLICK: More command button
    CHOOSE: Monitor status from the pop-up menu
    The Dial-Up Networking Monitor dialog box appears showing statistical performance summaries for the modem and for the current communications session. When you start a dial-up session, this monitor may be accessed by double-clicking its icon which appears in the taskbar.

11. To remove the dialog box:
    CLICK: Cancel command button

12. To end our tour of the Dial-Up Networking utility:
    CLICK: Close command button to remove the Dial-Up Networking dialog box
    CLICK: Close button ([✕]) on the "My Computer" window

QUICK REFERENCE
Adding a Phonebook Entry
for Dial-Up Networking

1. **DOUBLE-CLICK: "My Computer" icon ( )**
2. **DOUBLE-CLICK: Dial-Up Networking ( )**
3. **CLICK: New command button**
4. **Follow the steps in the New Phonebook Entry Wizard.**
5. **CLICK: Finish command button**

ACCESSING THE INTERNET

The Internet is a global network of approximately 11,000 independent computer networks, linking computers at educational institutions, scientific research centers, military establishments, government agencies, and corporate offices. These networks are connected by high-speed phone lines and special hardware, which makes it near impossible for you to connect directly to the Internet with a microcomputer. Most users will either connect to the Internet through their online service, such as The Microsoft Network, or through an Internet Service Provider (ISP), which provides Internet access for a fee.

As discussed in Session 1, the WWW provides a visual interface for the Internet and lets you search for information by clicking on hyperlinks. When you click a link, you are telling your web browser to retrieve a page from the Web. Each web page has a unique address called a *Uniform Resource Locator* or URL, such as http://www.irwin.com. With Windows NT 4.0, you already have everything you need to browse the Web. You can use the Dial-Up Networking utility to establish a connection to your ISP. Then, you launch the Microsoft Internet Explorer software, which is included free in NT, to retrieve and display web pages. To start the Internet Explorer (Figure A.5), double-click the Internet Explorer icon ( ) that appears on the desktop.

If you have not yet installed the software, you will see a Setup Microsoft Internet Explorer icon ( ) on your desktop instead. To install the software, you must insert the Windows NT installation CD-ROM and then double-click the Setup icon. Progress through the setup wizard to install the Internet Explorer.

MICROSOFT INTERNET
EXPLORER WINDOW

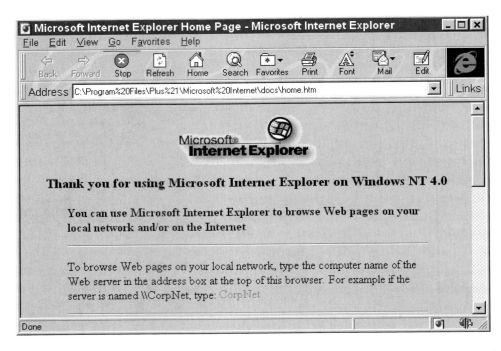

The Internet Explorer lets you manage e-mail messages, access newsgroups, and browse World Wide Web services based on HTTP, FTP, and Gopher. The features available in a web browser, whether Netscape Navigator or Internet Explorer, are relatively straightforward. To visit a new web site, you simply type in a URL in the text box provided near the top of the screen. You can also click the down arrow to view a list of recently visited web sites. Most tasks are easily accomplished using the toolbar buttons near the top of the screen. For more assistance, choose the Help, Help Topics command from the menu.

IN ADDITION ACCESSING HELP DIRECTLY FROM MICROSOFT

Using the Internet, you can keep current on product and company news by visiting Microsoft's web site. You'll also find helpful tips and online support for NT Workstation, NT Server, and other related products.

To access this information:

1. Establish an Internet connection.

2. CHOOSE: Help, Microsoft on the Web

3. CHOOSE: *a menu option* as shown at the right

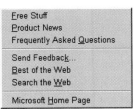

PEER WEB SERVICES

Like the Internet Explorer, NT Workstation includes Microsoft's Peer Web Services (PWS) software on the program installation CD-ROM. With NT Server, you will find the Internet Information Server (IIS) software on your CD-ROM. Using PWS running on NT Workstation, you can set up a small intranet for publishing personal web pages in a peer-to-peer environment. The NT Workstation license allows ten users to access your computer at a time, which is sufficient for testing and implementing an intranet. Like the Internet Information Server, PWS supports all the Information Server Application Programming Interface (ISAPI) extensions. However, you need NT Server and the IIS software to fully implement a Web site that supports FTP, HTTP, and Gopher services.

After installing the software as an Administrator, you access PWS from the Programs, Microsoft Peer Web Services (Common) command on the Start menu. On the cascading menu, choose the Internet Service Manager to view the running services. For more information on establishing a Peer Web Service for a workgroup, refer to the documentation that is installed with PWS.

SUMMARY

This session introduced you to some of the resource and communications utilities included with Windows NT. To begin the session, you learned how to use several network and disk administrative tools. After a brief description of setting up a modem, we described using Microsoft Exchange to send and receive e-mail. Next, you learned how to add a new entry to your Dial-Up Networking options. Finally, the session explored the World Wide Web using Microsoft Internet Explorer and Peer Web Services.

COMMAND SUMMARY

Many of the commands and procedures appearing in this session are provided in the command summary in Table A.2.

TABLE A.2	*Task Description*	*General Instruction*
Command Summary	Setting up a modem	Choose Settings, Control Panel from the Start menu and then double-click the Modems icon (). Follow the steps in the Install New Modem wizard.
	Setting up Microsoft Exchange and other services	In the Control Panel window, double-click the Add/Remove Programs icon (▦). Click the *Windows NT Setup* tab and then select the *Communications* check box and *Windows Messaging* check box.
	Compose a message	In Exchange, click the New Message button (✉) and then select the recipients using the To button. Fill in the subject header and body text and then click the Send button(✉).
	Send and receive messages	In Exchange, choose the Tools, Deliver Now command. Select the *Send Mail* and the Receive Mail check boxes and then click OK.
	Adding an entry for dial-up networking	Open the Dial-Up Networking utility by double-clicking the "My Computer" (🖥) icon and then double-clicking Dial-Up Networking (📠). Click the New command button and follow the steps in the New Phonebook Entry wizard.

KEY TERMS

backup
A duplicate copy of data from your hard disk that is typically stored on a separate medium, such as a tape, removable disk, or optical disk.

event
Any occurrence or activity that requires NT to notify the user. The three event categories include System, Security, and Application.

partitions
A storage area on a hard disk; *partitioning* prepares and segments a physical hard disk into usable storage areas by the operating system.

Remote Access Service (RAS)
A service that manages remote dial-in users and their permissions for running programs and accessing data on the network.

Index

The page numbers in boldface indicate Quick Reference procedures.